FREE THINGS FOR CAMPERS

and others who love the outdoors

FREE THINGS FOR CAMPERS

and others who love the outdoors

Jeffrey Weiss
Edited by Susan Osborn

A Perigee Book

Perigee Books
are published by
G. P. Putnam's Sons
200 Madison Avenue
New York, New York 10016

Copyright © 1982 by Jeffrey Weiss Group, Inc.
All rights reserved. This book, or parts thereof,
may not be reproduced in any form without permission.
Published simultaneously in Canada by General Publishing
Co. Limited, Toronto.

Edited by Susan Osborn
Text prepared by Tom Cowan
Design: Jeanette Vasquez
Research: Garin Wolf
Special thanks to Denise Van Lear, Janine Frontera,
Deborah Bracken, & Sam Mitnick

Library of Congress Cataloging in Publication Data

Weiss, Jeffrey.
Free things for campers.

"A Perigee book."
1. Camping—Equipment and supplies—Catalogs.
2. Free material—Catalogs. I. Title.
GV191.76.W44   1982   011'.03   81-15405
ISBN 0-399-50605-5   AACR2

First Perigee printing, 1982

Printed in the United States of America

CONTENTS

I. Introduction 7
II. Outdoor Gear: Clothes and Equipment 8
III. Outdoor Provisions 24
IV. Outdoor Places 37
V. Cyclists, the Modern Trail Riders 55
VI. Fishing and Boating 62
VII. Coping with the Outdoors 72
VIII. Conservation 101
IX. Enjoying the Outdoors 113
X. Tips for the Trailwise 127

All of the items listed in this volume were available at press time. While we and the suppliers have every hope that the items will be available through 1982, we cannot guarantee this.

I. Introduction

By Denise Van Lear, Associate Editor, *Backpacker* magazine

More than ever before, people are actively and regularly seeking the quiet splendors and manifold pleasures of the great outdoors. A highly rewarding excursion might materialize in a month-long trek or a brief jaunt in the woods an hour or so from the urban crunch.

Unlike so many other pursuits, the backcountry experience calls for simplicity, originality, and complete freedom from the toilsome demands of fashion, expensive lift tickets and admission fees, restaurants and hotels. What you carry in your pack allows you an independence unknown to the car-bound tourist. You are one of the lucky, smart souls who can cozy up to a tree or riverside and call it home.

Free Things for Campers was compiled for the trailwise individual who likes to get away from it all in style, and for free or *almost* free. In putting together this highly practical compendium, our *Free Things* specialists have scouted out hundreds of useful items and tips for broadening your backcountry horizons.

And what of the plethora of things you can acquire simply for the asking? Outdoor accessories, foods, books, and information sources abound, and if they're not free, they are fabulously inexpensive.

For a sampling, how would you like to make a rather serious study of wildlife management for only $2.00? *Free Things* tells you how. Or you could stock your library with educational fliers and books on hypothermia, coping with man-eating insects, cold-weather camping, a complete first-aid guide—all for free! You could become the chic-est chef in the neighborhood, whipping up such freeze-dried delectables as "Loch Ness stew" or "meadow mushroom soup," each under $1.40. Fish identification charts, topographical maps, ditty bags, seam sealers, soap dishes, sweetly scented biodegradable soaps, mugs, manufacturers' catalogs of still more outdoor paraphernalia—our findings are practically endless.

In clear and concise fashion, *Free Things for Campers* tells you what to look for, where to find it, and, most importantly, how to get it. Thanks to *Free Things*, you may find yourself entering a fascinating new world of outdoor pleasure.

II. Outdoor Gear: Clothes and Equipment

For the Hardy Mountaineer

Products from Black Ice are developed to withstand extreme temperatures and the most ruthless climatic conditions. Sleeping bags, outerwear, and tents are constructed of strongly insulated and protective materials to assure outdoors people that comfort and physical safety can be achieved with colorful, lightweight equipment.

Send: a postcard

Ask for: catalog

Write to: Black Ice
120 Woodland Ave.
Reno, NV 89523

Clothing and Equipment

Eddie Bauer designed and built America's first quilted goose-down jacket. Since then Eddie Bauer has been serving outdoors people with all types of clothing, equipment, and accessories. This catalog for 1982 will show you the most recent lines of accouterments for all types of outdoor recreational activities.

Send: a postcard

Ask for: 1982 catalog

Write to: Eddie Bauer
Fifth and Union
P.O. Box 3700
Seattle, WA 98124

Build Your Tipi

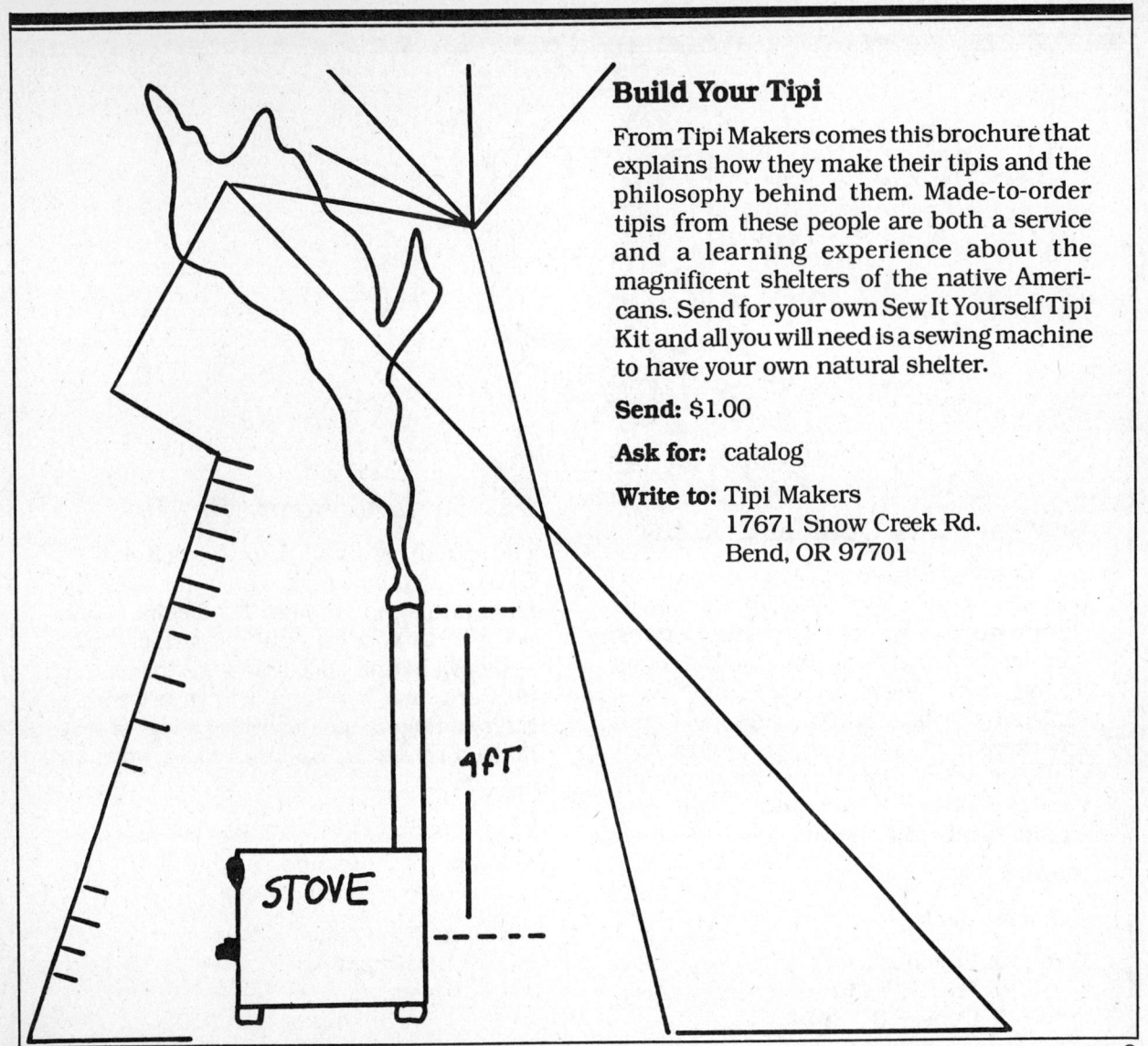

From Tipi Makers comes this brochure that explains how they make their tipis and the philosophy behind them. Made-to-order tipis from these people are both a service and a learning experience about the magnificent shelters of the native Americans. Send for your own Sew It Yourself Tipi Kit and all you will need is a sewing machine to have your own natural shelter.

Send: $1.00

Ask for: catalog

Write to: Tipi Makers
17671 Snow Creek Rd.
Bend, OR 97701

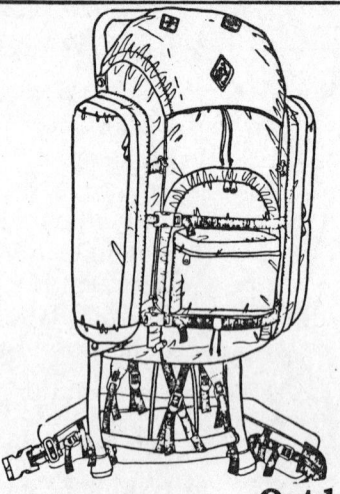

Sew Your Own Outdoor Clothing

The Frostline Kit is a complete, ready-to-sew package with all components included: precut quality fabric, all sewing notions, step-by-step instructions. You'll get big savings by making your own clothing, plus a sense of satisfaction that can't be bought anywhere. You can also personalize your clothing with distinctive monograms. Frostline puts the fun into sewing and eliminates the risk.

Send: a postcard

Ask for: catalog

Write to: Frostline Kits
Frostline Circle
Denver, CO 80241

Outdoor Equipment with Tips

The nice thing about this catalog from Don Gleason's is that there are tips for selecting tents and sleeping bags. The beginner will not have to wonder about the various styles and devices and not know what to look for. Here are some handy guidelines as well as a very complete mail-order catalog of the main brands in sporting and outdoor equipment.

Send: a postcard

Ask for: camping and backpacking equipment catalog

Write to: Don Gleason's Camper
Supply Co.
Pearl St.
Northampton, MA 01060

Folding Trailers

You see them up and down America's highways, bouncing along behind the cars that pull them. What you don't know is what they will look like when they are unfolded. Folding trailers come in so many sizes and with so many options today that if you are thinking of buying one, you ought to do some reading up first. This catalog is a good way to start. Inspect eight of Coleman's trailers and learn about the different parts and accessories.

Send: a postcard

Ask for: Coleman folding trailers catalog

Write to: The Coleman Co.
250 N. St. Francis
Wichita, KS 67201

Camp Supply and Expedition Catalog

Turn your desire for a wilderness experience into reality. But first start with this handy and complete mail-order catalog that will show you the many types of gear and equipment that are available for modern campers and hikers. Clothing, equipment, food, even books on the subject are available through the mail.

Send: $1.00

Ask for: expedition guide and catalog

Write to: Indiana Camp Supply Inc.
P.O. Box 344
Pittsboro, IN 46167

Bags, Pouches, Wallets

Rugged, waterproof panniers and bags are for people who like to bike and need convenient carriers for their food and supplies. This product catalog shows and describes the various panniers, bags, and wallets from Kangaroo Products. Bags that carry your books, rackets, or that strap on your bike. Wallets for your checkbook, key ring, sunglasses, and change.

Send: a postcard

Ask for: product catalog

Write to: Kangaroo Baggs
39 W. Main St.
Ventura, CA 93001

Tenting

For the latest styles and designs in tents, check out this glossy catalog from Johnson Wax Associates. Here you will discover the many shapes and structures that have been developed to provide shelter in any climate or season. From one-person pup tents to large, semi-permanent family tents, you'll be surprised at the latest technology for quick and easy tenting.

Send: 50¢

Ask for: catalog

Write to: Eureka Tent
P.O. Box 966-FT
Binghamton, NY 13902

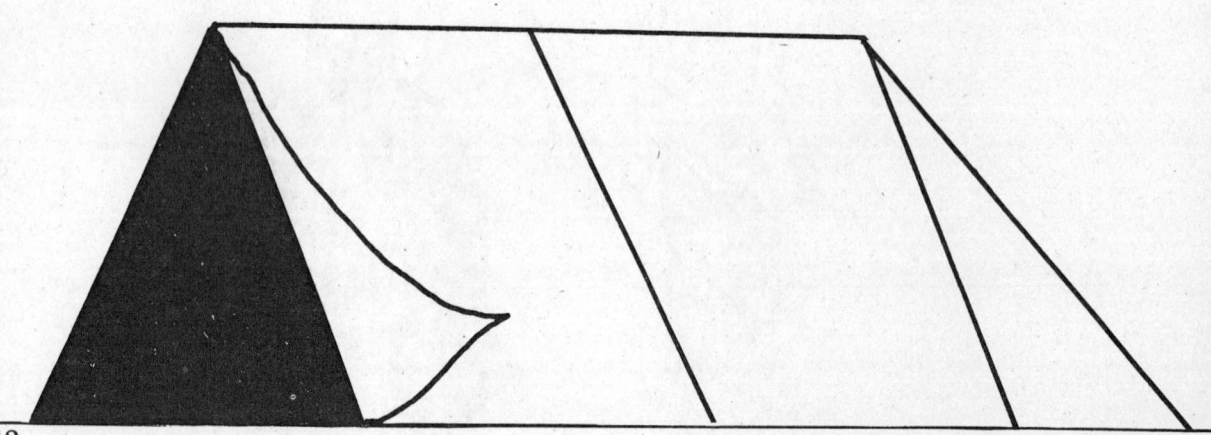

Outdoor Equipment

This free catalog from Bugtussle Outfitters will give you ideas for low-cost equipment for land or water excursions. Items include handmade hiking sticks, rescue lines, and nylon stuff bags.

Send: a postcard

Ask for: catalog

Write to: Bugtussle Outfitters
c/o Stan Cooper
Rt. #2, P.O. Box 231
Heiskell, TN 37754

Live in a Tipi

These tipi people have been making Sioux-style tipis for 25 years. Their tipis have been set up all over North America and parts of Europe and Asia. These tipis are modeled on authentic Sioux originals, with sloping backs to let the smoke out between the flaps and a backward slope that also makes the tipi more graceful in appearance. Send for this free catalog to inspect the designs and prices.

Send: a postcard

Ask for: Sioux Tipi order form

Write to: Goodwin-Cole Tentmakers
1315 Alhambra Blvd.
Sacramento, CA 95816

Outing Products

The basic products for a family outing have always been a major priority for the Coleman Co. Coolers, jugs, stoves, and lanterns—you can't really have an outing without them. Over the years the basic designs have remained the same, but each season there are new options and adaptations to make your outings more successful. Find out what the latest products are like from this handy catalog.

Send: a postcard

Ask for: Coleman outing products catalog

Write to: The Coleman Co.
250 N. St. Francis
Wichita, KS 67201

Old-Time Knives

This catalog will delight hunters and trappers who enjoy the look and feel of old-time knives. It lists over 70 knives, shears, and sharpening stones, not to mention gourmet cutlery. Each item is pictured, priced, and described.

Send: a postcard

Ask for: Old-Time Quality Knives catalog

Write to: Maher and Grosh
P.O. Box 120
Clyde, OH 43410

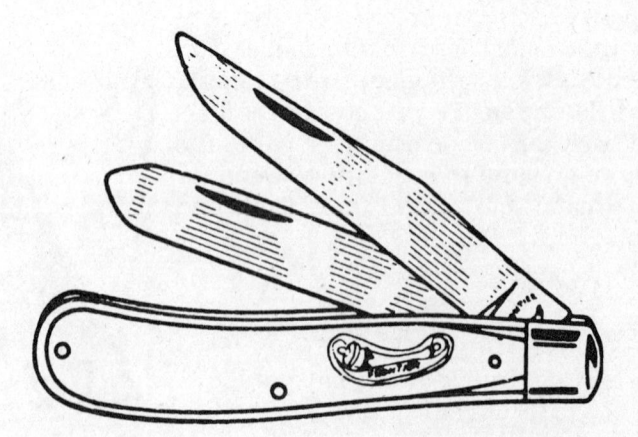

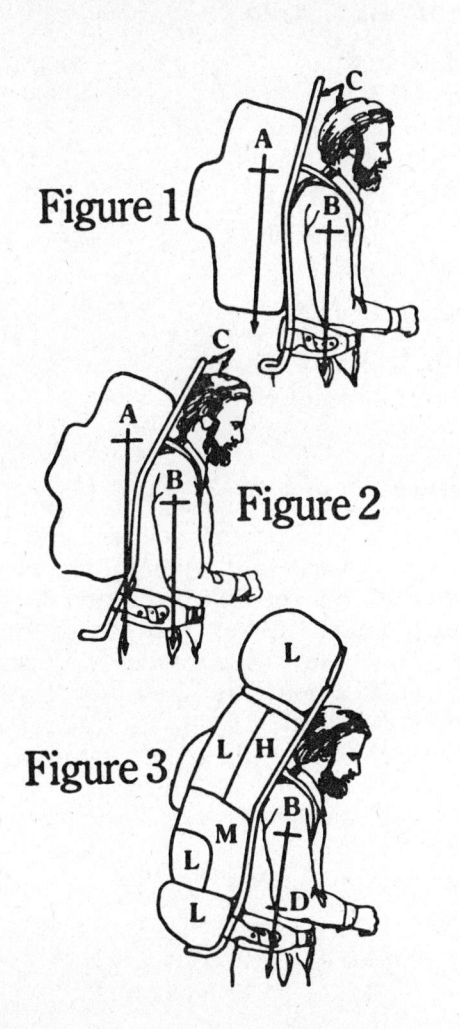

Outdoor Equipment

The pioneer spirit that developed the wilderness lives on in many outdoor enthusiasts. Conscientious people who love the outdoors will look for quality equipment and study the options before lugging the latest technology into nature's domain. Here is another catalog that will give you an overview of the many wilderness and outdoor products that are available for the modern pioneer.

Send: a postcard

Ask for: catalog

Write to: Canondale Co.
35 Pulaski St.
Stamford, CT 06902

Outdoor Gear

Not just a catalog of the latest items in the Jansport line, this handsome brochure also offers a wealth of technical information on framepacks, tents, and luggage. See the newest styles and learn how to make intelligent choices.

Send: 50¢

Ask for: catalog

Write to: Jansport
Paine Field Industrial Park
Everett, WA 98204

Wilderness Equipment

From the Great Pacific Iron Works comes this new catalog of hardware and software. Mountain-climbing equipment, ropes, carabiners, pulleys, straps, and slings as well as packs, jackets, shirts, shorts, and sweaters are listed. A very complete assemblage of everything you could want in clothing and accessories.

Send: $1.00

Ask for: catalog

Write to: Great Pacific Iron Works
P.O. Box 150
Ventura, CA 93002

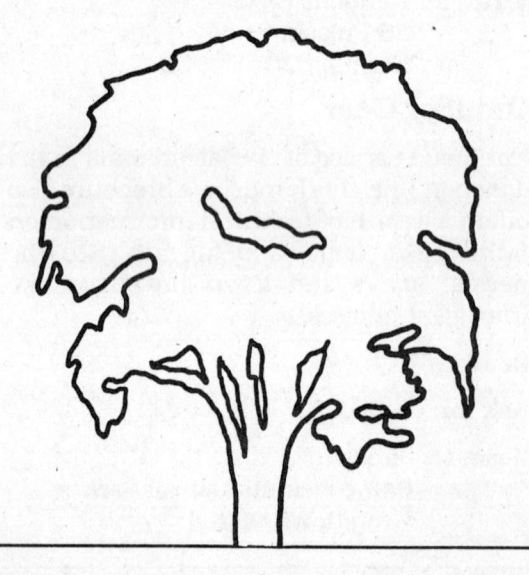

Camping Catalog

This camping and outdoors catalog from West Fork, Inc., has everything from scoop to nuts—tents, packs, clothing, accessories. Photos, sketches, descriptions, and prices help you decide. No handling or shipping charge on any item.

Send: a postcard

Ask for: catalog

Write to: West Fork, Inc.
211 Main St.
Lakefield, MN 56150

Homemade Country Things

This catalog of make-it-yourself kits will give you the materials and instructions for hand-making sensible, functional, and durable items, the way your grandparents did. These kits are made for people interested in *doing*, and then enjoying the results of their efforts. All sorts of things can be made at home, such as snowshoes, comforters, dulcimers, and canoes.

Send: $1.00

Ask for: kits catalog

Write to: Country Ways, Inc.
3500 Hwy. 101 South
Minnetonka, MN 55343

L. L. Bean

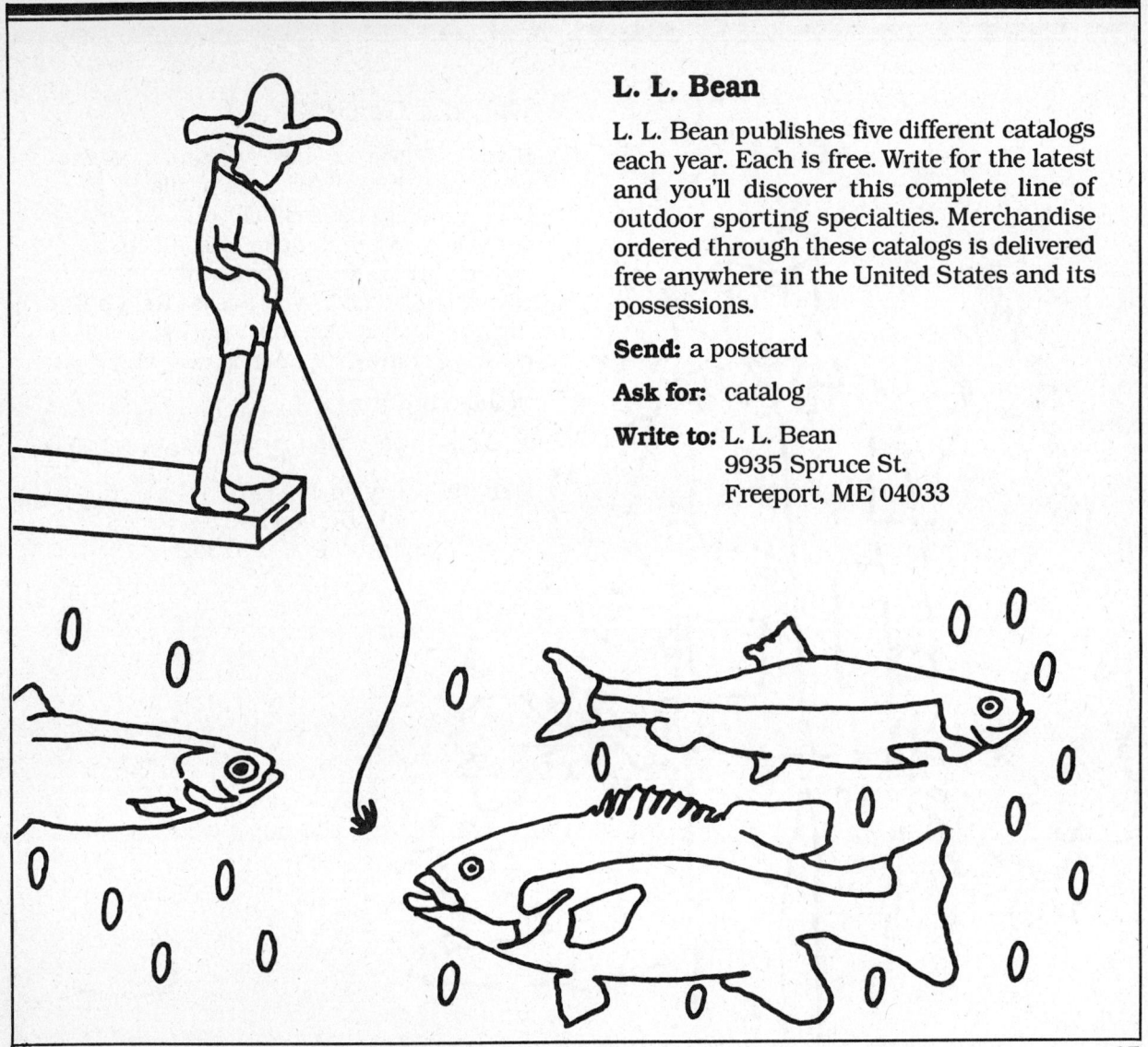

L. L. Bean publishes five different catalogs each year. Each is free. Write for the latest and you'll discover this complete line of outdoor sporting specialties. Merchandise ordered through these catalogs is delivered free anywhere in the United States and its possessions.

Send: a postcard

Ask for: catalog

Write to: L. L. Bean
9935 Spruce St.
Freeport, ME 04033

Outdoor Gear

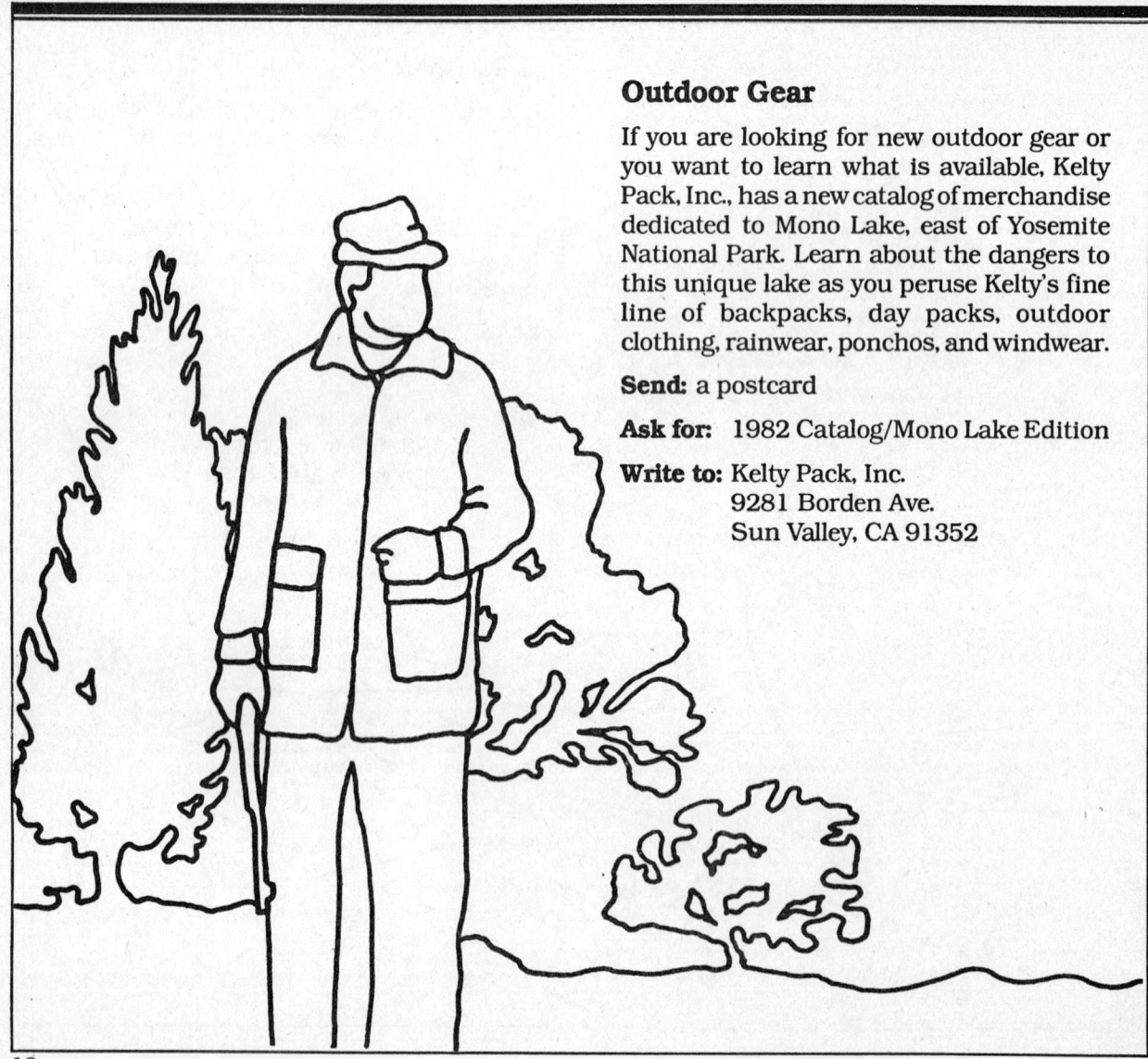

If you are looking for new outdoor gear or you want to learn what is available, Kelty Pack, Inc., has a new catalog of merchandise dedicated to Mono Lake, east of Yosemite National Park. Learn about the dangers to this unique lake as you peruse Kelty's fine line of backpacks, day packs, outdoor clothing, rainwear, ponchos, and windwear.

Send: a postcard

Ask for: 1982 Catalog/Mono Lake Edition

Write to: Kelty Pack, Inc.
9281 Borden Ave.
Sun Valley, CA 91352

Footwear

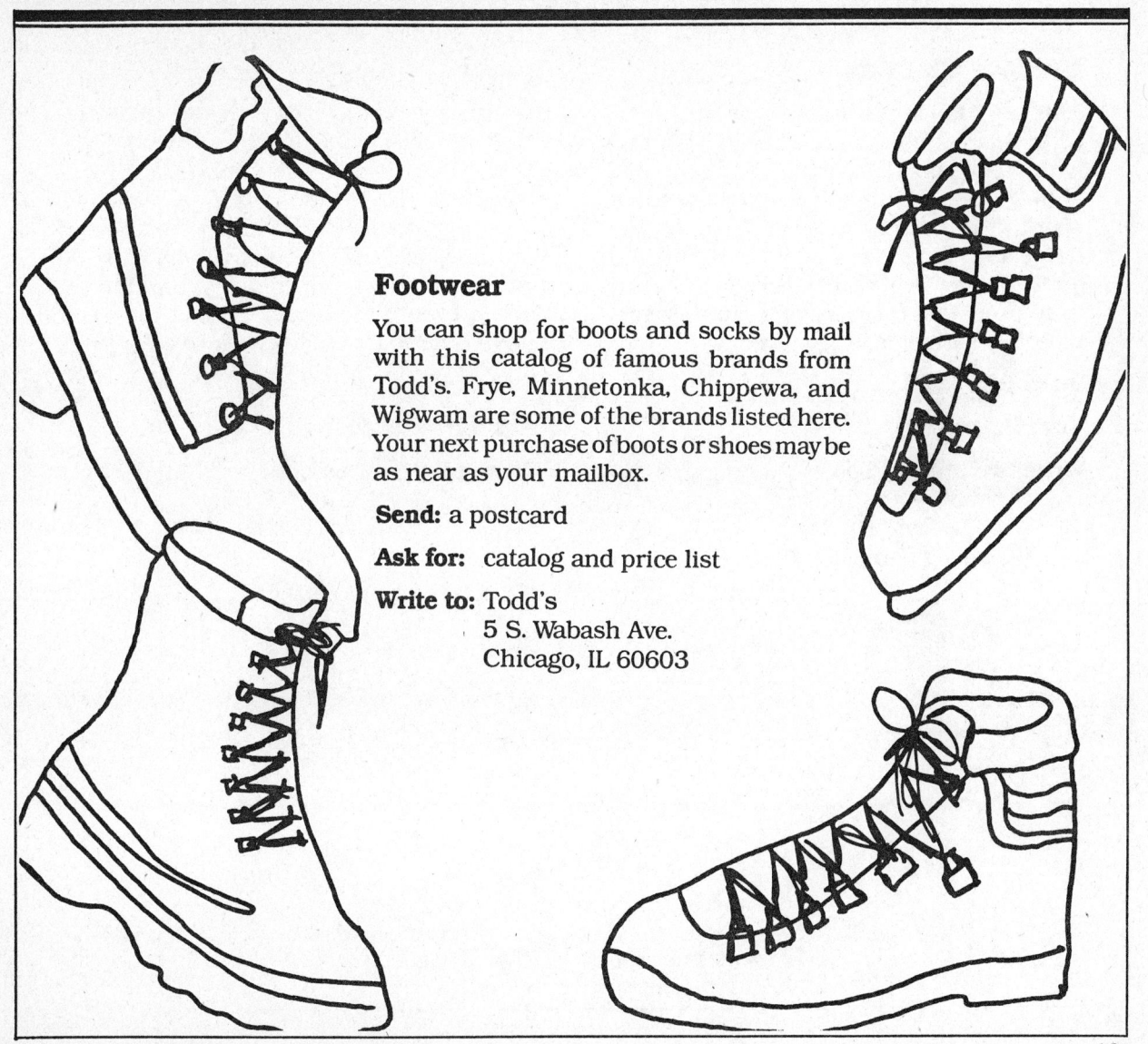

You can shop for boots and socks by mail with this catalog of famous brands from Todd's. Frye, Minnetonka, Chippewa, and Wigwam are some of the brands listed here. Your next purchase of boots or shoes may be as near as your mailbox.

Send: a postcard

Ask for: catalog and price list

Write to: Todd's
5 S. Wabash Ave.
Chicago, IL 60603

Outdoor Clothing

This big catalog of outdoor garments from Chinook Sport, Ltd., handsomely illustrated with color photographs of live models, shows you the latest in international sportswear. Each article of clothing can be inspected for color, style, and overall appearance. See the latest in skiwear, insulated jackets, thermal underwear, reflective garments, and more.

Send: $2.00

Ask for: catalog

Write to: Chinook Sport, Ltd.
550 E. Rogers Rd.
P.O. Box 1076
Longmont, CO 80501

Lost!

Whether you're lost or right on track, it's nice to plot your journey through the wilderness. Johnson Wax Associates has a complete line of compasses, pedometers, and altimeters. You can also get map cases of transparent plastic so that you can fold your map to the desired section, hang it around your neck, and not need to unfold it every time you want to check your location.

Send: 50¢

Ask for: catalog

Write to: Silva Compass
P.O. Box 966-FT
Binghamton, NY 13902

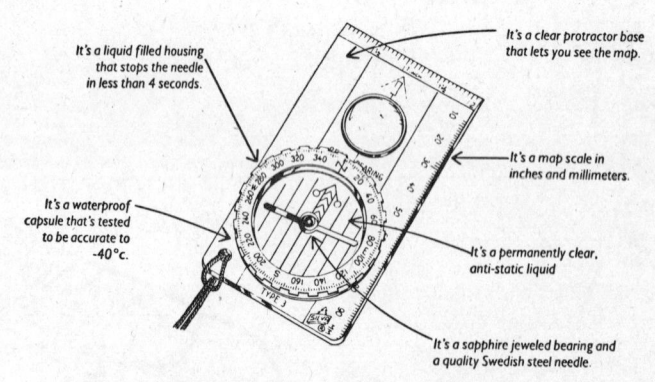

It's a liquid filled housing that stops the needle in less than 4 seconds.

It's a clear protractor base that lets you see the map.

It's a map scale in inches and millimeters.

It's a waterproof capsule that's tested to be accurate to -40°c.

It's a permanently clear, anti-static liquid

It's a sapphire jeweled bearing and a quality Swedish steel needle.

IT'S A SYSTEM OF FINDING YOUR WAY—AS SIMPLE AS 1-2-3

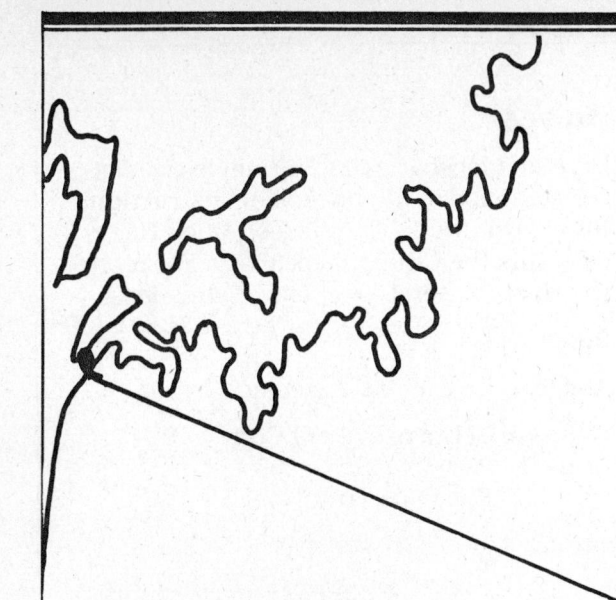

Tents

There is so much to look for when buying a tent. Ventilation, size, shape, materials, colors, ease of setting up—these are just a few of the considerations that should go into making a wise selection. If you are looking for big, roomy, traditional cabin-size tents for family camping, this catalog from Coleman will show how these reliable tents are constructed and how to use them.

Send: a postcard

Ask for: "Canvas Products 1982"

Write to: The Coleman Co.
250 N. St. Francis
Wichita, KS 67201

Outdoor Equipment

This 400-page full-color catalog from Bass Pro Shops covers everything an outdoors person would want for those long fishing and camping trips. Tents, coolers, sunglasses, augers, clothing, and a host of fishing equipment, including a make-your-own-worm kit. All items are manufactured by reliable companies.

Send: $2.00

Ask for: Bass Pro Shops catalog

Write to: Bass Pro Shops
P.O. Box 4046
Springfield, MO 65808

For the Hearty Backpacker

The ole knapsack on the back has come a long way since the army-green canvas pouch that outdoors people used to carry. Now they come in a wide assortment of colors, shapes, and sizes for adults and children alike. This sleek catalog from Johnson Wax Associates will show you the latest in backpacks so that you can select one that meets your personal needs. There is an entire world of zippers, snaps, pockets, and straps that can transport your food and supplies anywhere you want to go!

Send: 50¢

Ask for: catalog

Write to: Camp Trails
P.O. Box 966-FT
Binghamton, NY 13902

Knives

Here is a lockback that is completely rust-resistant and of rigid, durable construction. It's one you won't want to lose. Uncle Henry calls this the Ultimate Lockback. For more information, send for this free almanac.

Send: a postcard

Ask for: "Old Timer Almanac"

Write to: Schrade Cutlery Corp.
28 Canal St.
Ellenville, NY 12428

Trail Gear

The basics for any overnight hiking are backpack, sleeping bag, and tent. The Coleman Co.'s Peak One line of these items incorporates the latest technology to make your outdoor excursions as safe and enjoyable as possible. Also included are the latest models of lanterns and stoves, small, lightweight, and durable for backpacking ease.

Send: a postcard

Ask for: "1982 Trail Notes"

Write to: The Coleman Co.
250 N. St. Francis
Wichita, KS 67201

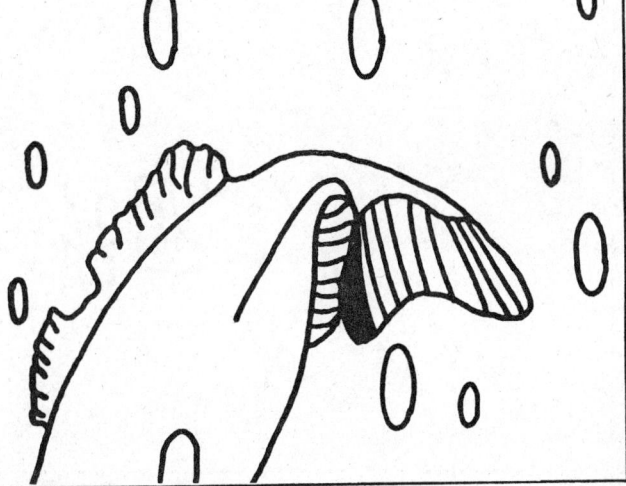

Wild Water Equipment

If you are going to raft the wild waters, you should have the correct gear, including the proper wet suits. This catalog contains life vests, sprayskirt kits, wet-suit kits, and bonnie hot pogies to keep your hands warm and dry even in cold water or on bitter days. Inspect these products meant to keep you warm and dry when the cold water drains you of body heat 35 times faster than cold air.

Send: a postcard

Ask for: Wildwater Designs catalog

Write to: Wildwater Designs Ltd.
230 Penllyn Pike
Penllyn, PA 19422

III. Outdoor Provisions

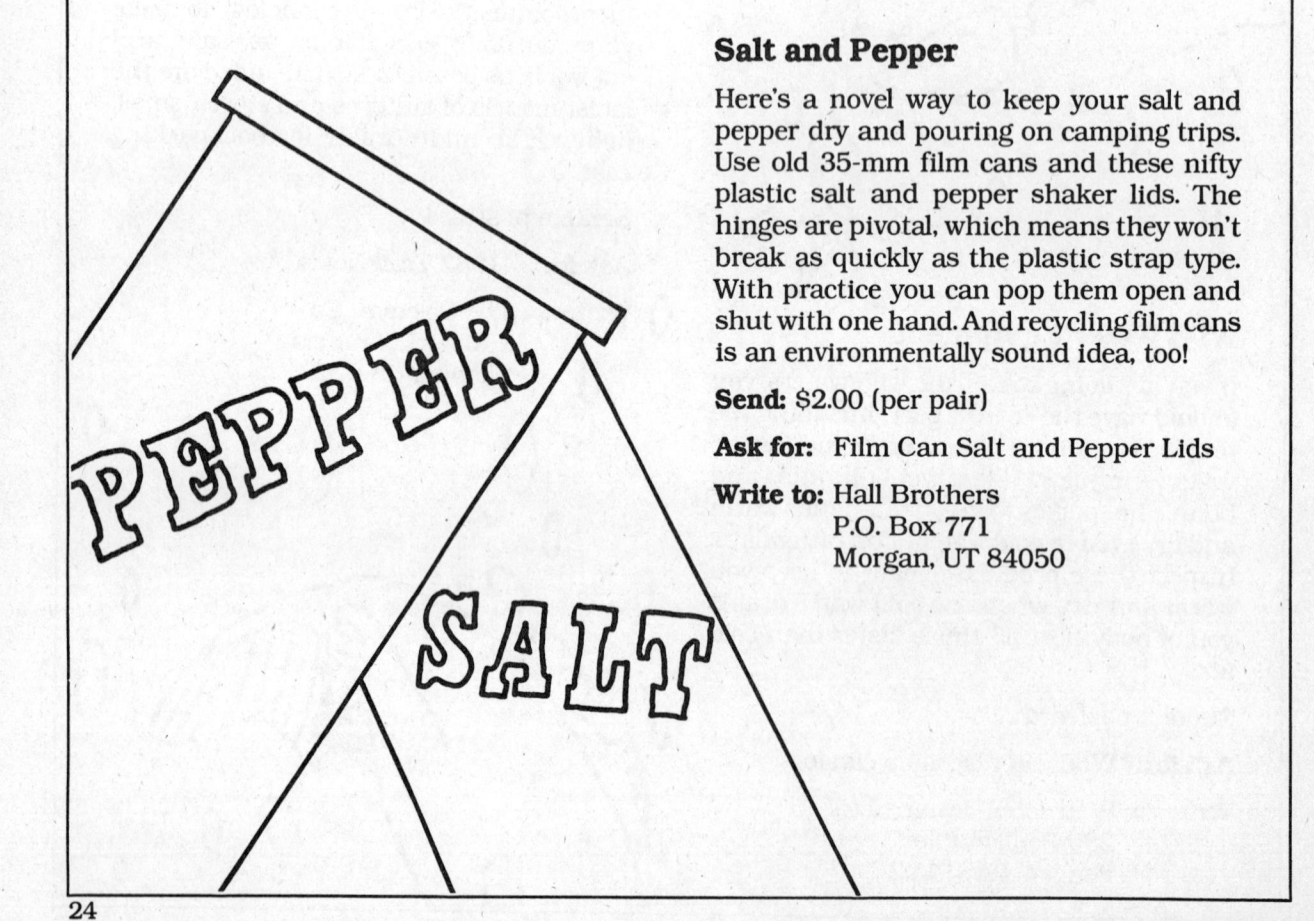

Salt and Pepper

Here's a novel way to keep your salt and pepper dry and pouring on camping trips. Use old 35-mm film cans and these nifty plastic salt and pepper shaker lids. The hinges are pivotal, which means they won't break as quickly as the plastic strap type. With practice you can pop them open and shut with one hand. And recycling film cans is an environmentally sound idea, too!

Send: $2.00 (per pair)

Ask for: Film Can Salt and Pepper Lids

Write to: Hall Brothers
P.O. Box 771
Morgan, UT 84050

Squeeze Tubes

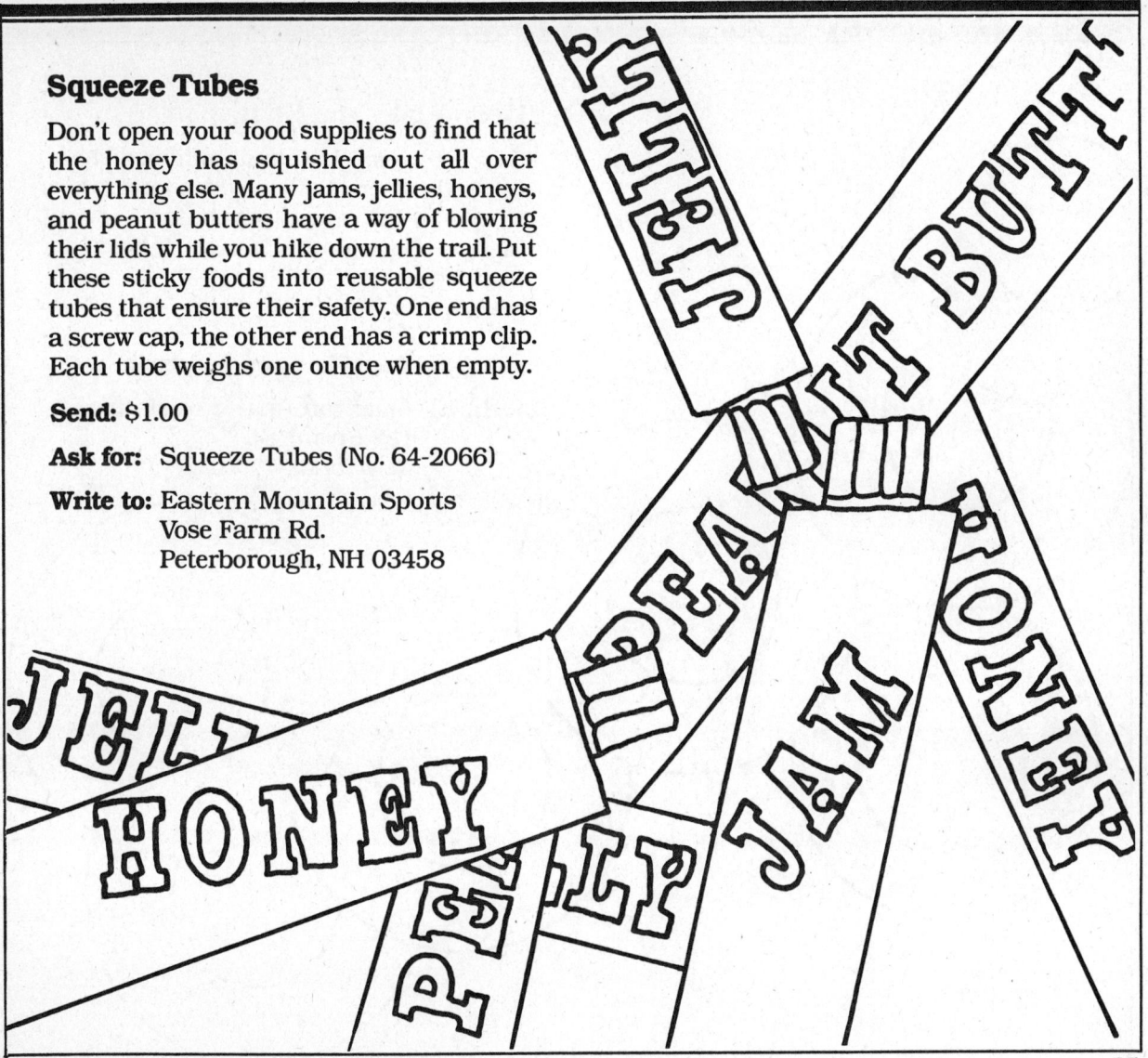

Don't open your food supplies to find that the honey has squished out all over everything else. Many jams, jellies, honeys, and peanut butters have a way of blowing their lids while you hike down the trail. Put these sticky foods into reusable squeeze tubes that ensure their safety. One end has a screw cap, the other end has a crimp clip. Each tube weighs one ounce when empty.

Send: $1.00

Ask for: Squeeze Tubes (No. 64-2066)

Write to: Eastern Mountain Sports
Vose Farm Rd.
Peterborough, NH 03458

Deep Plate and Saucepan

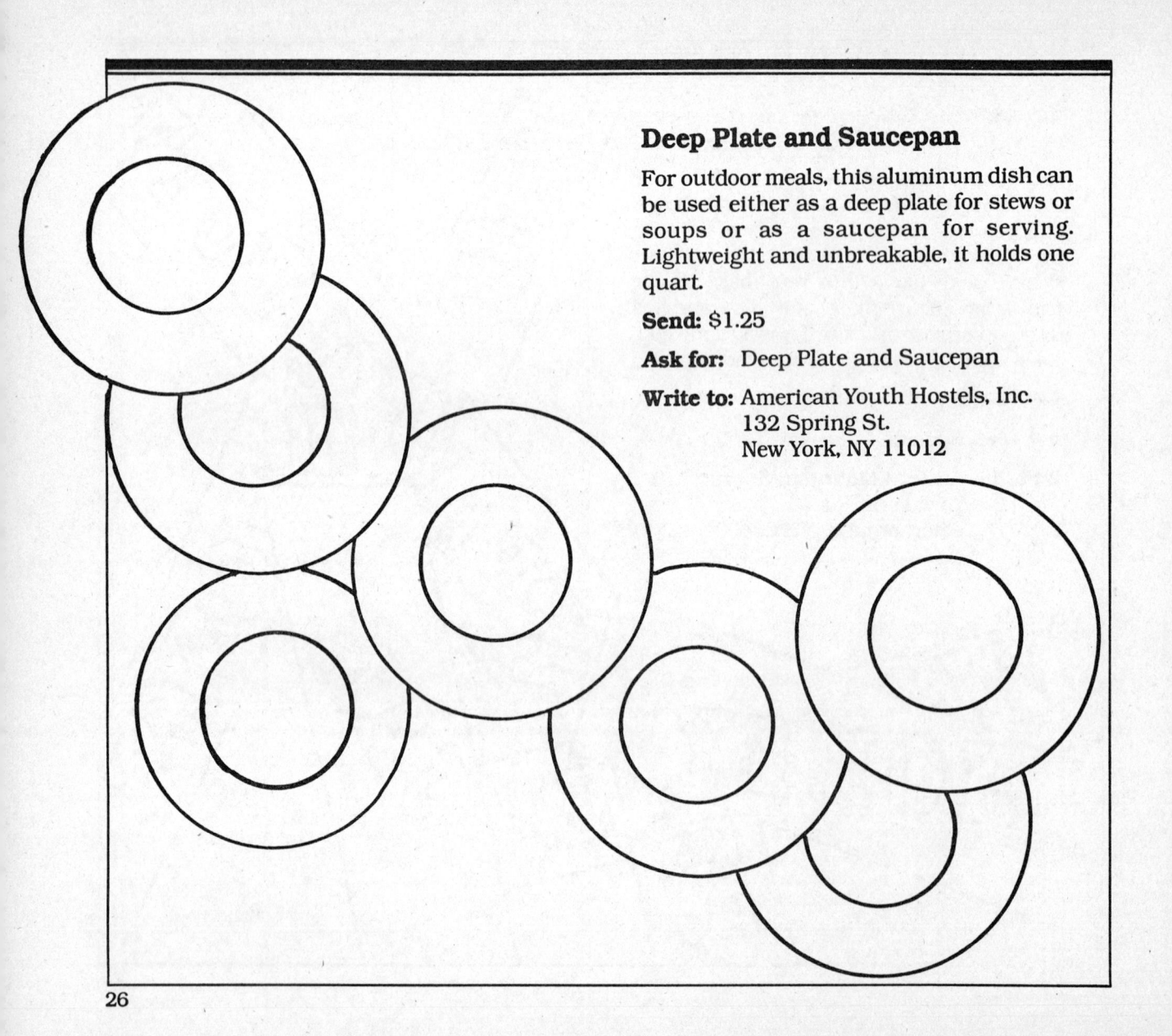

For outdoor meals, this aluminum dish can be used either as a deep plate for stews or soups or as a saucepan for serving. Lightweight and unbreakable, it holds one quart.

Send: $1.25

Ask for: Deep Plate and Saucepan

Write to: American Youth Hostels, Inc.
132 Spring St.
New York, NY 11012

Pot Gripper

You don't have to buy pots and pans with long, cumbersome handles that make packing for an extended trip frustrating. Get this clever little pot gripper and you'll be able to remove any pot or pan from a hot fire without burning yourself. It clamps tightly onto the lip of pots and pans. Easy to operate with one hand. Save your fingers from getting scorched.

Send: $1.50

Ask for: Lightweight Pot Gripper (No. 64-6828)

Write to: Eastern Mountain Sports
Vose Farm Rd.
Peterborough, NH 03458

Natural Food Backpack Dinners

Meals in one pot, quick cooking, all natural. These nutritious meals are generous and tasty and can be cooked on the trail or at home. They're excellent introductions to whole-grain cooking for those who have never tried it before. For hikers, these meals are packaged in polyethylene bags for easy disposal.

Send: a postcard

Ask for: leaflet

Write to: Natural Food Backpack Dinners
P.O. Box 532
Corvallis, OR 97330

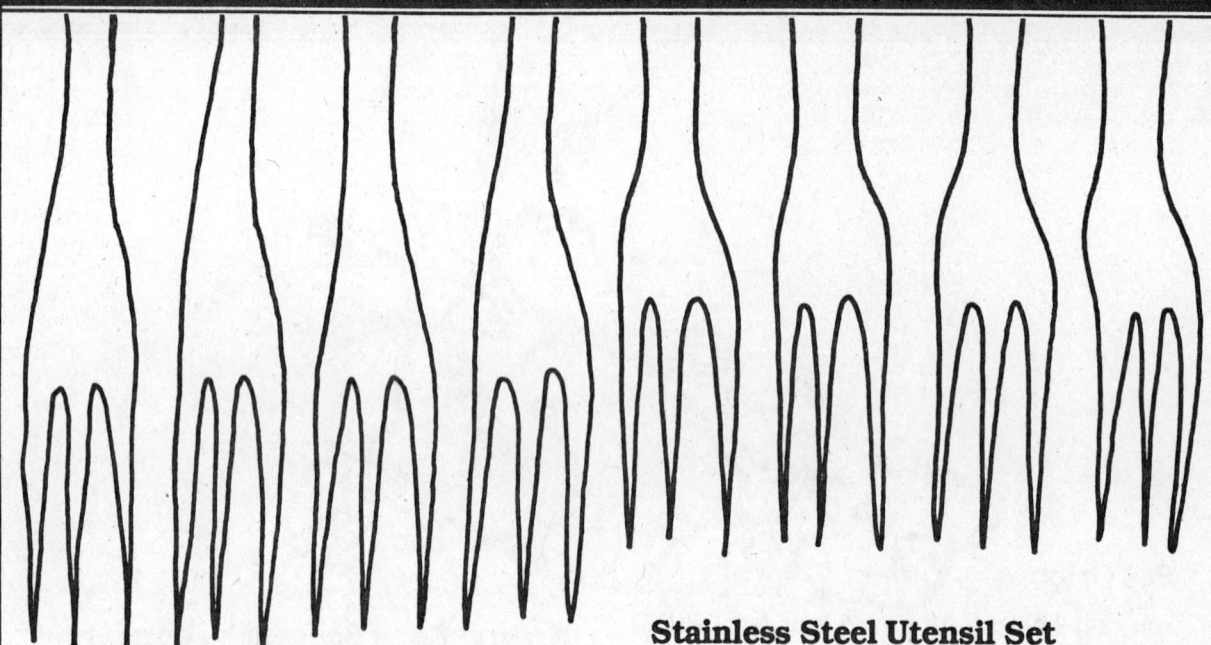

Chow Set

Add to your forest cutlery with this three-piece set: fork, knife, and spoon. All are stainless steel and nest in a plastic case. Good for backpacking because total weight is only .16 lb.

Send: $1.30

Ask for: Three-piece Chow Set (No. 443)

Write to: Moor and Mountain
63 Park St.
Andover, MA 01810

Stainless Steel Utensil Set

Get a knife-fork-spoon set for every member of your camping party. Each can carry this stainless steel set in its convenient plastic case. The entire ensemble collapses into the 7½"-by-1¾"-by-1" package. Weighs only three ounces. Handy for backpacks.

Send: $1.50

Ask for: Stainless Steel Utensil Set (No. 64-6166)

Write to: Eastern Mountain Sports
Vose Farm Rd.
Peterborough, NH 03458

Backpacking Cookery

This cookbook from the National Outdoor Leadership School has grown out of years of organizing backpacking expeditions into far-flung regions of the country. It contains helpful rationing lists, food charts, and other dietetic information needed by two people for 10 days. The appendix contains an equivalency table of common backpacking foods.

Send: $1.95

Ask for: "NOLS Cookery"

Write to: Emporia State Press
ESU Box 43
1200 Commercial
Emporia, KS 66801

Folding Ladle

Don't let your soups and stews get cold while you bail them out with teaspoons. You can take this 1½-ounce soup ladle with you. It folds up small enough to fit in the palm of your hand or inside a drinking cup. Ideal for serving from dishes that are too big or hot to pass around.

Send: $1.99

Ask for: Folding Ladle (No. 6212)

Write to: Early Winters, Ltd.
110 Prefontaine Place South
Seattle, WA 98104

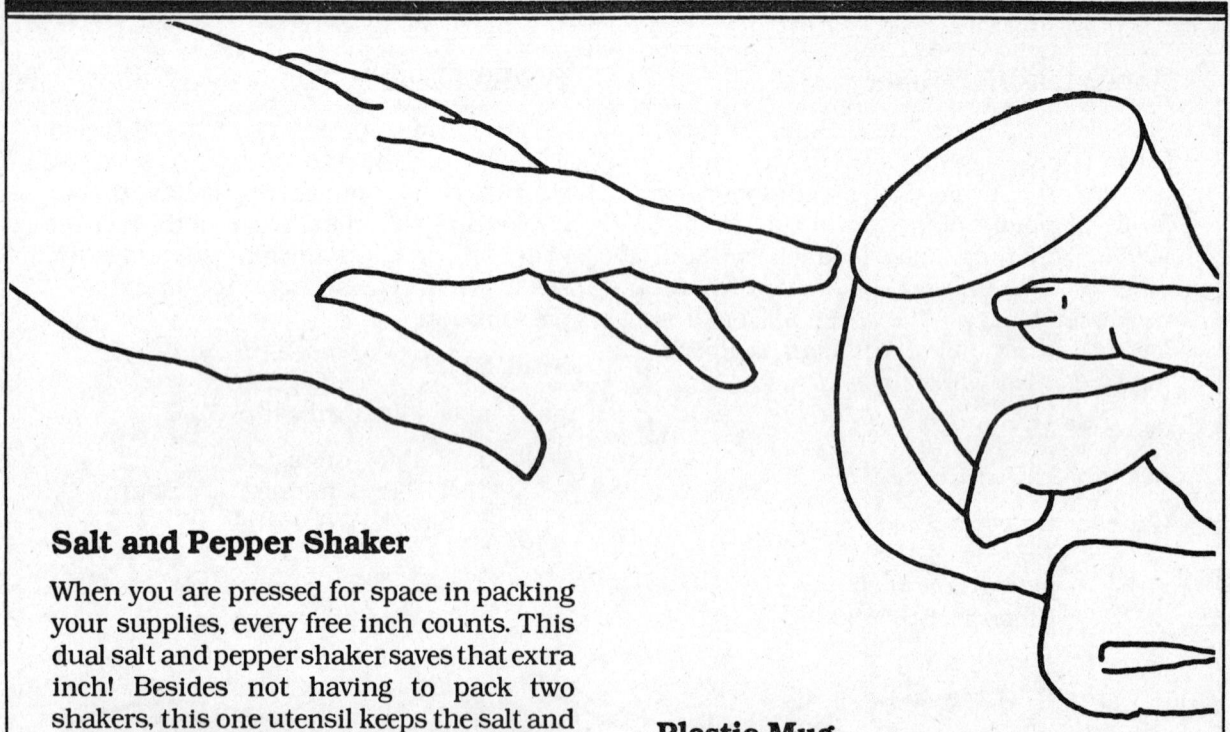

Salt and Pepper Shaker

When you are pressed for space in packing your supplies, every free inch counts. This dual salt and pepper shaker saves that extra inch! Besides not having to pack two shakers, this one utensil keeps the salt and pepper together in one place so you always know where the other is. The pepper side is black and the salt side is white, so you won't make mistakes.

Send: 69¢

Ask for: Plastic Salt and Pepper Shaker (No. 64-6729)

Write to: Eastern Mountain Sports
Vose Farm Rd.
Peterborough, NH 03458

Plastic Mug

This unbreakable mug will not melt when brimming with your favorite hot beverage. Made of semi-rigid plastic, this hardy cup is great for either outdoor or indoor use.

Send: 50¢

Ask for: Plastic Mug

Write to: American Youth Hostels, Inc.
132 Spring St.
New York, NY 10012

G.I. Can Opener

Less than 2″ long, this can opener is the real McCoy, not an imitation. Handy, convenient, easy to use, weighs only two ounces.

Send: 29¢

Ask for: G.I. Can Opener (No. 64-6968)

Write to: Eastern Mountain Sports
Vose Farm Rd.
Peterborough, NH 03458

Trail Lunches

Eating nutritious meals on the trail is always a problem if you don't plan ahead and include quick, light lunches. From Dri-Lite's Backpacker's Pantry come three Kwik Lunches, each containing fruit bar, trail cookies, and hard candy. Lunch One: Beef Jerky. Lunch Two: Beef Jerky and Peanut/Chocolate Munch. Lunch Three: Beef Sausage Stick.

Send: $2.00

Ask for: Kwik Lunch One (#161)

Send: $1.95

Ask for: Kwik Lunch Two (#162)

Send: $1.75

Ask for: Kwik Lunch Three (#163)

Write to: Dri-Lite Foods, Inc.
630 Twin View Blvd.
Redding, CA 96003

Emergency Foods

For information on foods and foodstuffs that will last over long-term storage, write to Northeast Survival Products. You never know when your cabin, boat, or backpack will run out of food. Keep extra supplies that will last for a long, long time.

Send: a postcard

Ask for: free catalog for emergency food

Write to: Northeast Products
P.O. Box 428
Dept. FTP
Monticello, NY 12701

Plastic Compartment Plate

Weighing only three ounces, this three-compartment plastic plate is 9" in diameter. It's ideal for backpacking trips when it is essential to keep your pack weight to a minimum.

Send: 85¢

Ask for: Plastic Compartment Plate

Write to: American Youth Hostels, Inc.
132 Spring St.
New York, NY 10012

Gourmet Outdoor Soup

Pack a little elegance into your knapsack for your next trip. Dining around a campfire doesn't have to be all beans and hash! These six delicious gourmet soups are premeasured and easy to fix. They're naturally flavored, ready for you to add water and simmer over your fire. Specify the flavors you want when ordering: mock turtle, cockie leekie, mulligatawny, French onion, Senegalese, or potato leek.

Send: 85¢ each

Ask for: Gourmet Outdoor Soup
(No. 0730)

Write to: Early Winters, Ltd.
110 Prefontaine Place South
Seattle, WA 98104

Coffee on the Trail

Now you can enjoy the aroma and taste of fresh coffee wherever you are! These individual foil packets, each sealed under nitrogen, keep coffee fresh up to one full year. Don't plan your next overnight without these handy brew bags. Specify Louisiana Dark, Colombian, or Decaff when ordering.

Send: $1.00 (for five bags)

Ask for: Coffee Bags (No. 0701)

Write to: Early Winters, Ltd.
110 Prefontaine Place South
Seattle, WA 98104

Camping Foods

This catalog from Stow-a-Way will introduce you to the world of freeze-dried and dehydrated foods. Handy for lightweight, economical meals. Also covered in the 64-page catalog are the accessories you will need for camping with these easy-to-store and -carry foods: containers, carriers, mixers, pouches, stoves...even vitamins. You will also receive a sample of Stow-Lite Fruit Galaxy.

Send: $2.00

Ask for: 1982 catalog

Write to: Stow-a-Way Industries
166 Cushing Hwy. (Rt. 3A)
Cohasset, MA 02025

Egg Carrier

Everyone knows why eggs are so often not included on camping menus. They break! But with this sturdy plastic container you can carry a half dozen eggs safely. This rigid case has internal support structure for each egg and a snap closure. It is made to take eggs up through large size. Now you can pack eggs and find them still in one piece for those hearty campfire breakfasts that smell and taste so good.

Send: $1.00

Ask for: Plastic Egg Carrier (No. 64-2124)

Write to: Eastern Mountain Sports
Vose Farm Rd.
Peterborough, NH 03458

Trail Foods

This simple order form from Trail Foods gives you a vast selection of Mountain House, Dri-Lite, Rich-Moor, and Alpineaire dehydrated and freeze-dried foods. Trail Foods offers a 17%–29% discount off suggested retail price.

Send: 50¢

Ask for: catalog

Write to: Trail Foods Co.
P.O. Box 9309
North Hollywood, CA 91609

Chocolate Break

Chocolate is fun to eat on the trail and good for a quick lift because it is an energizer. But it's not fun if it has melted inside your pocket or pack. Now you can hike on the hottest summer days and not have to worry about sticky chocolate oozing into places where you don't want it. This one-ounce Hershey bar resists melting even in August.

Send: 35¢

Ask for: Hershey's Tropical Chocolate (No. 61-1806)

Write to: Eastern Mountain Sports
Vose Farm Rd.
Peterborough, NH 03458

Game Recipes

Muskrat Meat Loaf, Roast Beaver, Fried Beaver, or Fried Pheasant. Sound mouth-watering? If so, send for this booklet of game recipes from Michigan. Cooking and serving game (by candlelight can be quite romantic!) is an art. After all, you have to know how to soak a muskrat overnight to get it properly seasoned.

Send: a postcard

Ask for: game recipes

Write to: Dept. of Natural Resources
P.O. Box 30028
Lansing, MI 48909

Mini-Spatula

This short 6½" mini-spatula weighs only one ounce and is made of plastic that won't scratch Teflon pan linings. A knurled alloy handle makes it easy to grab hold of as you flip omelets or pancakes on those chilly mornings around the breakfast fire. Don't ruin your eggs and pancakes with fork flipping! Flip it right—with a spatula.

Send: $1.95

Ask for: German Mini-Spatula (No. 6208)

Write to: Early Winters, Ltd.
110 Prefontaine Place South
Seattle, WA 98104

IV. Outdoor Places

Olympic National Park

This magnificent area on the northwest coast offers the true lover of the outdoors a veritable gold mine of geological wonders. Created by the sea, the rain, the mountains, and volcanoes, this wildlife area offers exciting adventures from its snowcapped mountain peaks to its rugged shoreline. This wall-sized map offers a geographic and geologic description for anyone interested in spending some time there.

Send: a postcard

Ask for: Olympic National Park Map

Write to: Olympic National Park
600 E. Park Ave.
Port Angeles, WA 98362

Petrified Forest

If you're planning to go to northern Arizona or just dreaming about it, you'll enjoy these offers from the Petrified Forest Museum. A large, 32-page, beautifully photographed book explains the story behind the scenery from prehistoric times to the present. A geologic cross-section map that follows Interstate 40 will let you learn about the various rock layers and geological formations as you whizz across the state. Or, if you decide to drive through the park itself, the park's discovery map will give you things to think about and places to go as you discover these natural and man-made wonders on your own.

Send: $1.50

Ask for: "Petrified Forest, the Story Behind the Scenery"

Send: $1.00

Ask for: Ask for: "I-40 Geological Cross Section Map"

Send: $1.00

Ask for: "Petrified Forest Discovery Map"

Write to: Petrified Forest Museum Assoc.
P.O. Box 277
Petrified Forest National Park
AZ 86028

A Vacation in Yellowstone

If you are planning a vacation to Yellowstone, you should have this free vacation guide to help you make your trip through the world's first national park a memorable one. Learn before you get there about the many fascinating natural wonders the park has to offer. Then go. And enjoy a breathtaking experience.

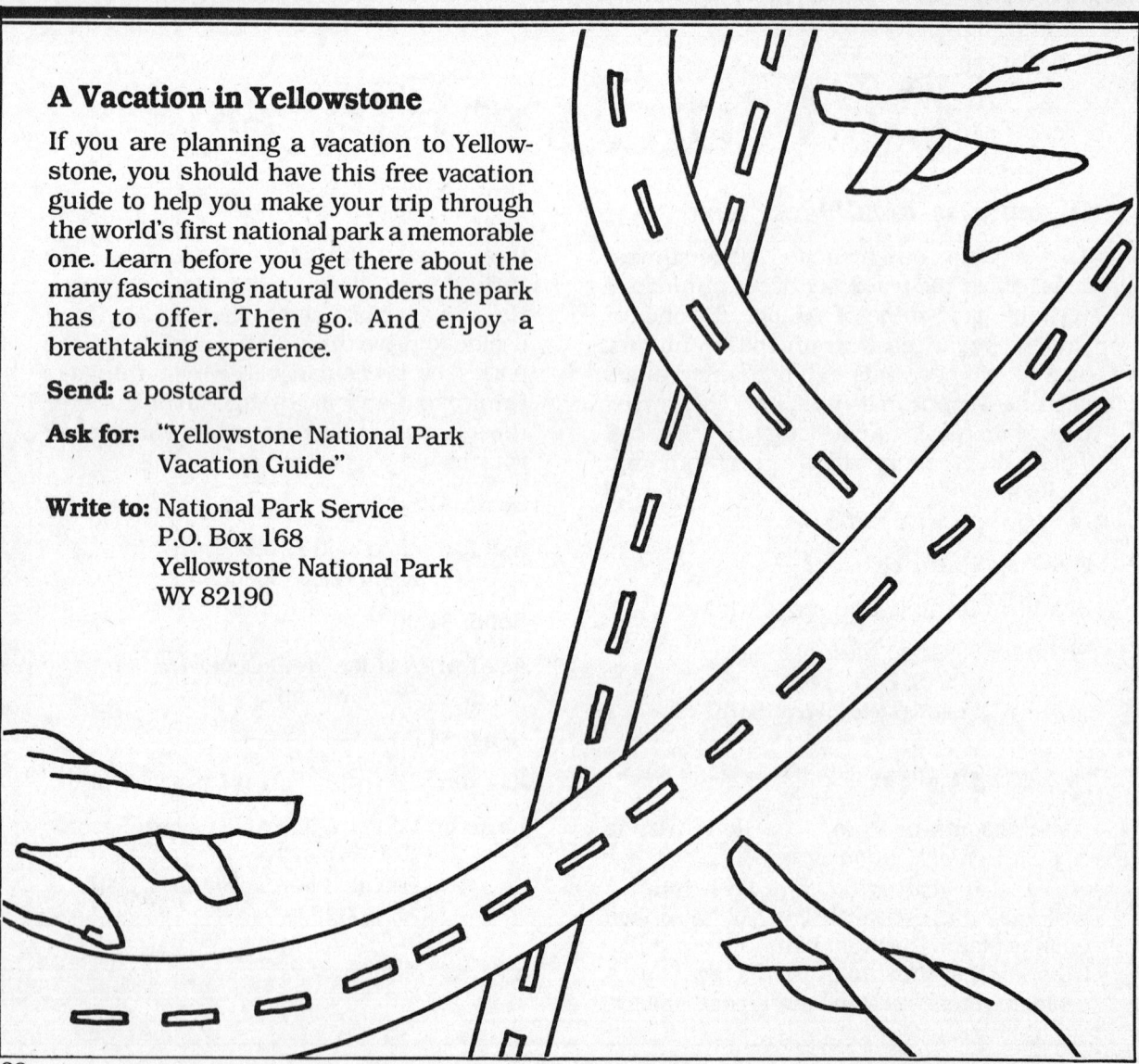

Send: a postcard

Ask for: "Yellowstone National Park Vacation Guide"

Write to: National Park Service
P.O. Box 168
Yellowstone National Park
WY 82190

Minnesota's Natural Resources

Did you know that the northern pike is one of two pike family members native to Minnesota and that it thrives in all regions of the state? Do you know the many factors that influence the behavior of the elusive walleye? Questions like these and more are covered in the DNR Reports, a series of free publications on Minnesota's natural resources published and distributed by the state's Department of Natural Resources. Write for a list of titles available in the series.

Send: a postcard

Ask for: list of the DNR Reports

Write to: Bureau of Information and Education
350 Centennial Office Building
St. Paul, MN 55155

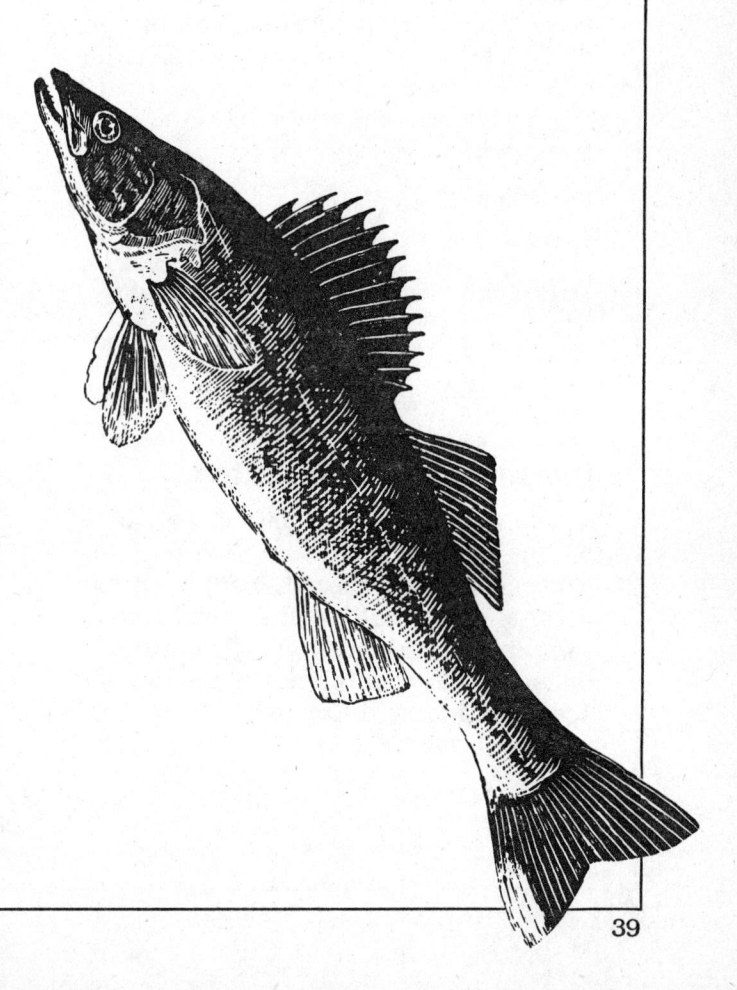

White-Water Rafting

Some of the best white-water rafting east of the Mississippi is in the Maryland, West Virginia, Pennsylvania area where the Cheat, Youghiogheny, and Gauley rivers beckon amateurs and professionals alike for thrills and excitement. A pamphlet from one of the oldest outfitters in the region will give you schedules, prices, tips, and hints for yourself or your group.

Send: a postcard

Ask for: white-water rafting brochure

Write to: Mountain Streams and Trails Outfitters
P.O. Box 106
Ohiopyle, PA 15470

Rivers and Trails Outfitters

Before you launch out, plan your canoe, hiking, or bike trip with easy-to-read, up-to-date maps from Rivers and Trails Outfitters in the Maryland and Virginia area. Maps for canoeing the basin of the Potomac and Shenandoah rivers, hiking the Appalachian Trail, and biking the C and O Canal Towpath are available.

Send: a postcard

Ask for: maps

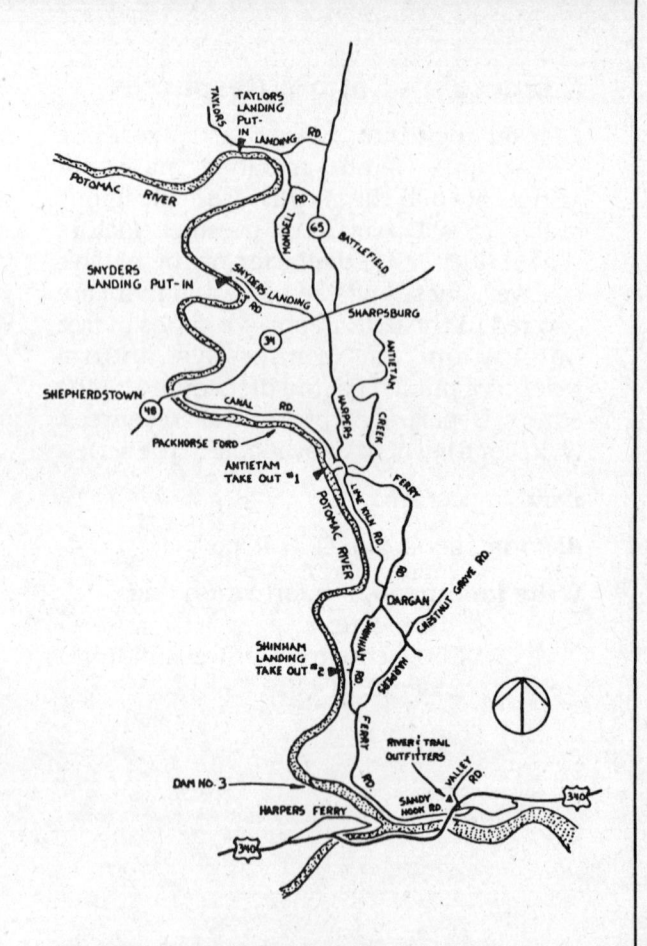

Write to: Rivers and Trails Outfitters
P.O. Box 246
Valley Road
Knoxville, MD 21758

Glacier National Park

For armchair naturalists and visitors to this unique park that bridges both the United States and Canada, this packet of maps, color photos, and wildlife and woodlore information is a must. Stretching from Alberta down into Montana, this gorgeous parkland will thrill all those who love breathtaking beauty and the natural wonders of the Rockies.

Send: a self-addressed, stamped envelope

Ask for: "About Bears"
catalog of publications
International Peace Park Map
park accommodations

Write to: Glacier Natural History Assoc.
Glacier National Park
West Glacier, MT 59936

Camping in Acadia

If you are interested in camping in Maine's Acadia National Park, you'll want this complete travel pack. Here you'll find trail maps, park regulations, and a checklist of the many birds in the park and what seasons to find them. Also included is a small pamphlet describing the park and showing the many features of this intriguing archipelago that will keep you returning year after year.

Send: a postcard

Ask for: Acadia Park Brochure

Write to: National Park Service
Acadia National Park
RFD #1, P.O. Box 1
Bar Harbor, ME 04609

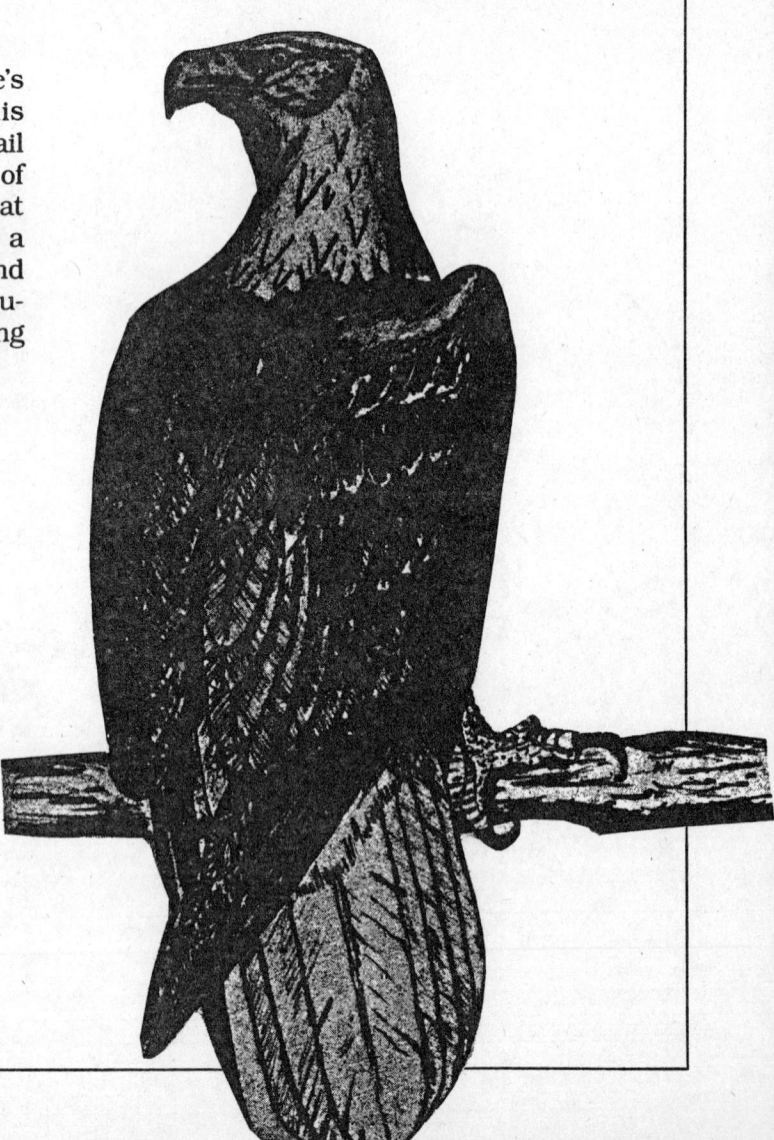

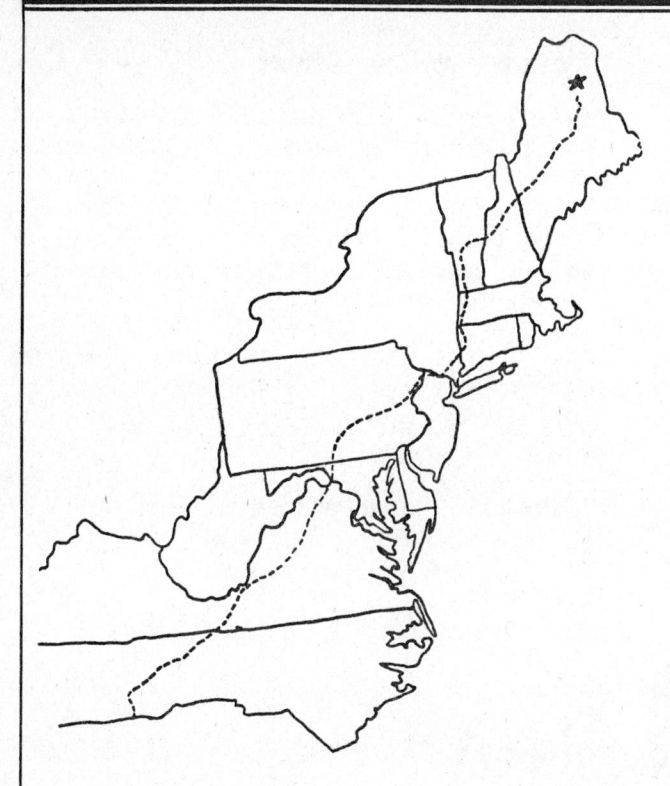

Appalachian Trail

From Maine to Georgia, the Trail offers experiences as rich and varied as the land, animal, plant, and bird life that it covers. The Trail is a living, breathing legacy for all concerned Americans who love the outdoors. This brochure will help you plan your hike on the Trail, give you the basic information, and tell you what you need to get started.

Send: a postcard

Ask for: brochure

Write to: "Appalachian Trail Conference"
P.O. Box 236
Harpers Ferry, WV 25425

Coastal Maps and Charts

The National Oceanic and Atmospheric Administration publishes nautical charts and miscellaneous maps for people engaged in outdoor boating, fishing, and sailing activities. The catalogs for these various charts, and maps are free. All you have to do is write for them.

Send: a postcard

Ask for: Map and Chart Catalog 5
Nautical Chart Catalog 1

Write to: National Oceanic and
Atmospheric Administration
National Ocean Survey (C-44)
Riverdale, MD 20840

Colorado Mountain Guide

If you are planning to climb any of Colorado's 14,000-foot peaks, be sure you are using the latest guidebook. Changes in land ownership, roads, trails, campsites, and climbing routes necessitate your having the most up-to-the-minute information. This condensed guide is a must.

Send: $2.00

Ask for: "The Colorado Fourteens, A Condensed Guide"

Write to: The Colorado Mountain Club
2530 W. Alameda Ave.
Denver, CO 80219

Yellowstone in Winter

Hiking, camping, or just driving through the Yellowstone country in winter? You should have this handy map and information booklet about winter services, accommodations, and snowmobile trails. Since not all restaurants and shelters are open, you should know which ones are and where they are.

Send: a postcard

Ask for: "Winter Guide to Yellowstone Country"

Write to: National Park Service
P.O. Box 168
Yellowstone National Park
WY 82190

Flathead National Forest

The wild and rugged Flathead National Forest has a wealth of outdoor activities for people of all ages. Send for these three pamphlets and forest travel map. The Hungry Horse Reservoir Recreational area is a paradise for fishermen, swimmers, and boaters. For backpackers, the Jewel Basin hiking area contains some of the most scenic and adventurous country available. The Danny On Trail was created to give the average hiker a five-mile walking tour of the high country with points of interest regarding the plant and animal life designated along the way.

Send: a postcard

Ask for: Flathead National Forest map
"Hungry Horse Reservoir Recreation Area"
"Danny On Memorial Trail"
"Jewel Basin Hiking Area"

Write to: Flathead National Forest
P.O. Box 147
Kalispell, MT 59901

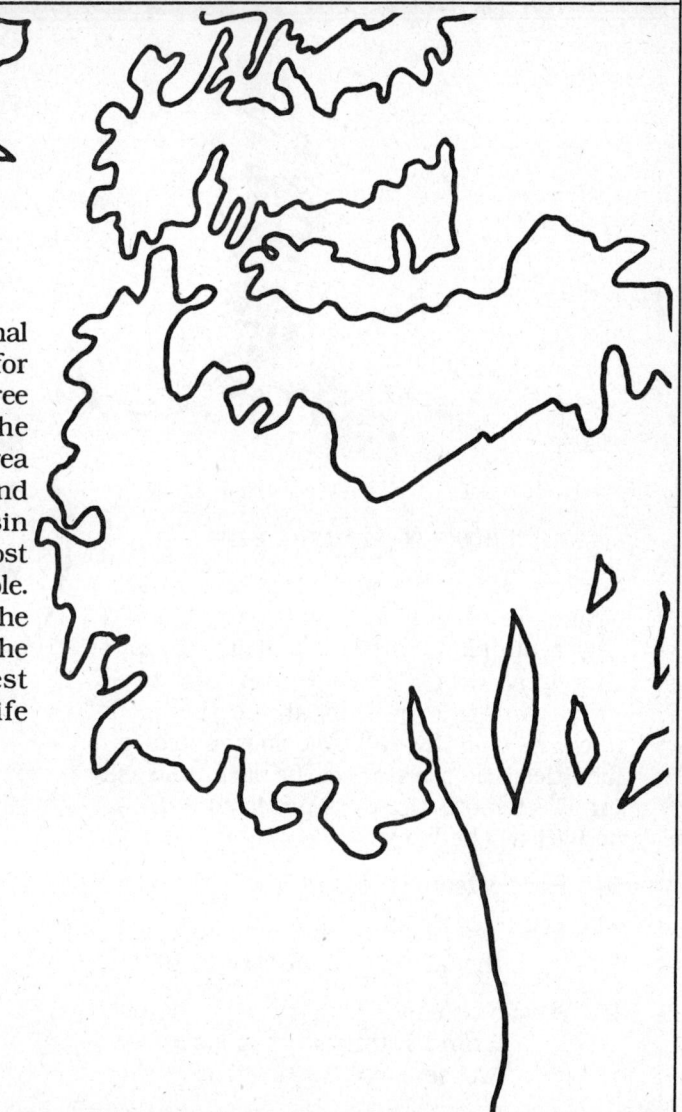

Grand Teton National Park

For an outdoor season in the majestic Grand Teton National Park, you should begin your plans with this wall-sized map of the area, which includes on the back important information about the park itself: its wildlife, trails, outdoor recreation facilities, and the story of the park. Also ask for "Teewinot," the park guide containing activities schedules.

Send: a postcard

Ask for: Grand Teton National Park map
the latest issue of "Teewinot"

Write to: National Park Service
Grand Teton National Park
Moose, WY 83102

Maryland's State Parks

Maryland is a small state, but its topography stretches through a great variety of contrasts. Coastal regions along the Chesapeake, the Piedmont Plateau area, and the spectacular Appalachian Mountains are sitting there waiting for you. Send for this free leaflet, which will acquaint you with the parks and forests that comprise this old, historic state in the mid-Atlantic.

Send: a postcard

Ask for: "Maryland: the Mountains, the Bay, the Ocean"

Write to: Maryland Park Service
Tawes State Office Building, B-2
Annapolis, MD 21401

Voyageurs National Park, Minnesota

Water dominates the Voyageurs National Park landscape. Within its boundaries are 30 lakes—some huge, some small. Bogs, marshes, and beaver ponds abound. Canoe and camp in the territory first opened up by French trappers and traders. This colorful map shows the extent of the park and gives useful information about what to expect—like black bears. The park is the home of 200 to 300 of them.

Send: a postcard

Ask for: Voyageurs map

Write to: National Park Service
Voyageurs National Park
P.O. Box 50
International Falls, MN 56649

The Grand Canyon

There are three separate areas in the Grand Canyon Park: the South Rim, the North Rim, and the Inner Canyon or Inner Gorge. Each has different facilities, different activities, and even different climates. Learn about the many attractions in one of America's most spectacular natural vacation spots. Send for the Grand Canyon map and the pamphlets dealing with hiking trails at the Grand Canyon.

Send: a postcard

Ask for: Grand Canyon map and hiking pamphlets

Write to: National Park Service
Grand Canyon National Park
Grand Canyon, AZ 86023

Ski Touring

The entire Flathead Forest is open for ski touring. Very few trails or roads are marked, so the choice is up to you. This guidebook will describe the various areas for skiing; each is ranked in terms of difficulty. Also included in this booklet are tips for cross-country skiers.

Send: a postcard

Ask for: "Ski Touring on the Flathead"

Write to: Flathead National Forest
P.O. Box 147
Kalispell, MT 59901

Florida

There's more in Florida than just sun and sand. This map of Florida's state parks, recreation areas, museums, ornamental gardens, and special features like historic, archaeological, and geological sites will surprise you. There's a lot to go for in Florida!

Send: a postcard

Ask for: "Florida State Parks"

Write to: Department of Natural Resources
Marjorie Stoneman Douglas Bldg.
3900 Commonwealth Blvd.
Tallahassee, FL 32303

Pacific Crest Trail

The Pacific Crest National Scenic Trail extends 2,600 miles from Canada to Mexico. If you are going to hike it in California, this colorful guide will show you the mapped area you'll be going through and some of the natural wonders you'll encounter along the way. With a guide divided into northern and southern sections and a central section that covers the Sierra Nevada, you'll be able to make decisions about your trip quite easily. Each section lists addresses of national parks and forests to write to for more information.

Send: a postcard

Ask for: "Pacific Crest Trail: California Section"

Write to: Office of Information
Pacific Southwest Region
USDA-Forest Service
630 Sansome St.
San Francisco, CA 94111

Outward Bound Programs

Outward Bound is a worldwide organization providing wilderness experiences of all types that are physically and psychologically challenging. Outward Bound has many free pamphlets describing various programs and courses. People of all ages have benefited through the self-discovery and new wilderness skills they have acquired from these real-life adventures. Write to Outward Bound and request information on the type of experience you are interested in or for general information about the many courses offered.

Send: a postcard

Ask for: Outward Bound pamphlets

Write to: Hurricane Island Outward Bound
P.O. Box 429
Rockland, ME 04841

Adventures Around the World

If you would like to volunteer to study flowers in a South American jungle, dig through archaeological ruins in Scotland, study prehistoric man in Spain, or do oceanographic research off the Gulf Coast, Earthwatch is for you. This 10-year-old program matches lay volunteers with field scientists to go anywhere in the world to study, research, explore. Send for this brochure and see for yourself the exciting and varied trips that are available. Then become a member of Earthwatch and set out!

Send: a postcard

Ask for: catalog

Write to: Earthwatch
10 Juniper Rd.
P.O. Box 127
Belmont, MA 02178

Winter Sport

Winter Sports in California

This brochure will inform you about the many types of winter sports available in "sunny" California—skiing, sledding, hiking, ice fishing, snowmobiling, skating, snow camping, and snowplay, not to mention hot springing. Find out where to enjoy these activities, what they cost, what kind of gear you'll need. A special section called "Planning Your Trip" will make the preparations easy.

Send: a postcard

Ask for: "Winter Sport in the National Forests of California"

Write to: Office of Information
Pacific Southwest Region
USDA-Forest Service
630 Sansome St.
San Francisco, CA 94111

Wilderness Journeys

Capture the spirit of the Old West on one of these many wilderness adventures through terrain that a little over a century ago was certainly no vacation. Today the West is tame and there are enjoyable and thrilling trips by horseback, by raft, and on foot. This brochure will familiarize you with the trips that are available and the type of equipment you will need. Arizona, Colorado, Wyoming, New Mexico, and Utah—see these states… and experience them…as pioneers once did.

Send: a postcard

Ask for: "American Wilderness Experience Trip Guide"

Write to: American Wilderness Experience
P.O. Box 1486
Boulder, CO 80306

Rugged Expeditions

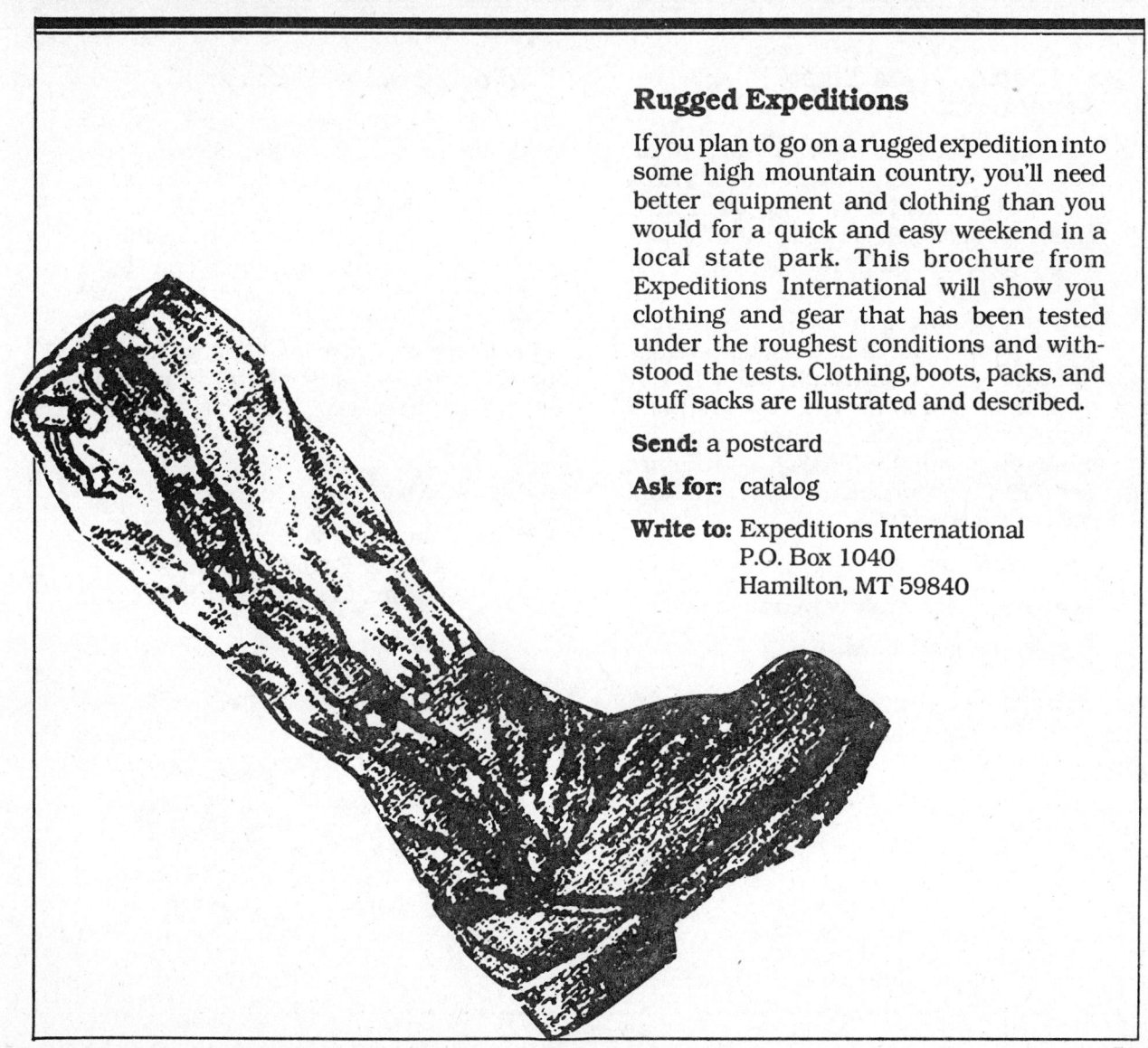

If you plan to go on a rugged expedition into some high mountain country, you'll need better equipment and clothing than you would for a quick and easy weekend in a local state park. This brochure from Expeditions International will show you clothing and gear that has been tested under the roughest conditions and withstood the tests. Clothing, boots, packs, and stuff sacks are illustrated and described.

Send: a postcard

Ask for: catalog

Write to: Expeditions International
P.O. Box 1040
Hamilton, MT 59840

Old-Time Wagon Train Adventures

Take a vacation on horseback and in an authentic covered wagon down trails through lonesome yet lovely canyons, across brush-covered high desert hills in rough and rugged Nevada. Trails lead through parts of the Forty Mile Desert, to Indian Lake or Ragtown, to the Wild Horse Corrals, and to Fort Churchill. Travel peacefully through scenic countryside, cover two or three miles a day, sit and sing around a campfire at night just as early settlers and pioneers used to do. Write for more information about these wagon train and pack horse adventures.

Send: a postcard

Ask for: Wagon Train Adventures leaflet

Write to: Dean Calkins
C-Bar-D Ranch
P.O. Box 902
3010 Hillsboro
Fallon, NV 89406

Exploring the Wilderness

The American Wilderness Alliance offers a wide series of explorations through the wilderness by a wide variety of means: skiing, horseback riding, hiking, rafting, sailing, dorying, sportyaking, canoeing. In addition, there are special programs such as photography workshops and educational trips. Send for this photographically illustrated brochure of the many trips available. Dates, prices, what to bring…and what surprises to expect are fully explained.

Send: 25¢

Ask for: "Wilderness Adventures"

Write to: American Wilderness Alliance
4260 E. Evans Ave., Suite 8
Denver, CO 80222

Wilderness in California

If you're wondering where the wilderness is in California and what you can do in it once you are there, this brochure is for you. How to plan your trip, no-trace camping, wilderness travel safety, campfire safety, facts about bears, and ways to get wilderness permits are all explained in detail. The wilderness! It offers something for everyone.

Send: a postcard

Ask for: "Wilderness in the National Forests in California"

Write to: Office of Information
Pacific Southwest Region
USDA–Forest Service
630 Sansome St.
San Francisco, CA 94111

Vermont's Long Trail in Winter

Planning to hike the Long Trail in winter? Be sure you know about hypothermia, frostbite, and dehydration. Take care to winterize your clothing and equipment. This vital brochure on winter hikes through the Green Mountains will tell you all this in addition to facts about the unwinterized trails, shelters, lodges, and even winter rainstorms. You'll also appreciate the charts of daily temperatures and average snow depths.

Send: a postcard

Ask for: "Winter Trail Use in the Green Mountains"

Write to: The Green Mountain Club, Inc.
P.O. Box 889
43 State St.
Montpelier, VT 05602

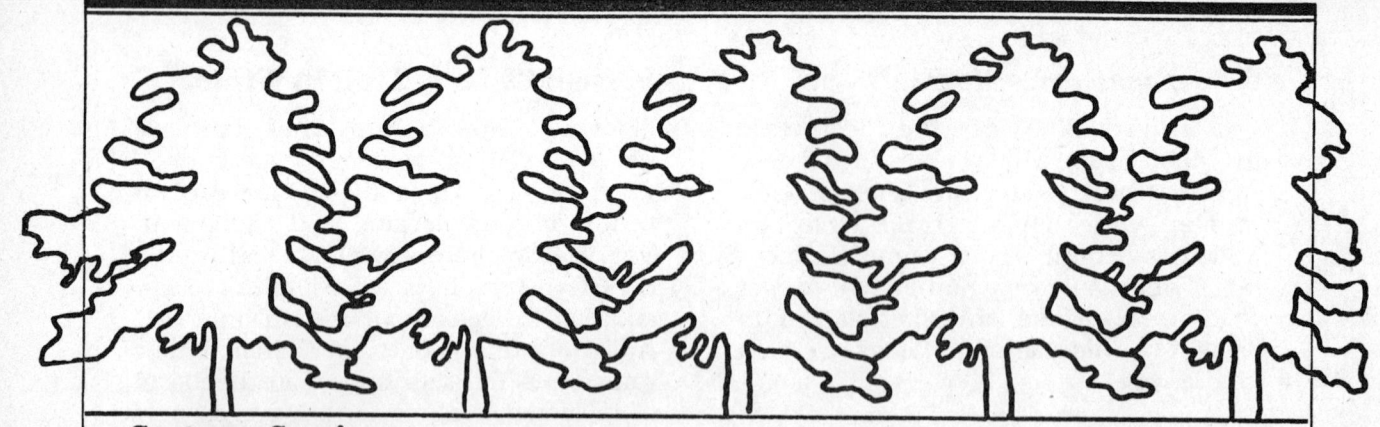

Summer Seminars

The outdoor classroom in the Grand Tetons offers seminars on all aspects of the fabulous environment contained within the Grand Teton Park: archaeology, birds, nature photography, mammals, flora, animal behavior, and more. College credit is available for these courses amidst 13,000-foot mountain peaks, jewellike lakes, and active glaciers. Further your education in this relatively untouched and intact ecosystem of marvelous beauty.

Send: a postcard

Ask for: Grand Teton Summer Seminars

Write to: Grand Teton Environmental
Education Center
Teton Science School
P.O. Box 68
Kelly, WY 83011

Map of Yellowstone

This beautiful wall map of Yellowstone National Park is a geyser of information as well as a map. On the back are photos and descriptions of dangerous animals; canyons, lakes, and mountains; geysers and hot springs; and a brief history of the Indians, mountain men, and explorers who traipsed through here in times gone by.

Send: a postcard

Ask for: map of Yellowstone

Write to: National Park Service
P.O. Box 168
Yellowstone National Park
WY 82190

V. Cyclists, the Modern Trail Riders

Tire Patching Kit

Even the most experienced bikers have flats sometime or other—and usually when they are least convenient. Don't get caught flat and patchless. Keep a generous supply of vulcanized patches and cement handy for those unlucky moments when you're all set to go but your bicycle isn't. Each order comes packed in a compact plastic box for easy carrying.

Send: $1.25

Ask for: Rema F-2 Patch Kit

Write to: American Youth Hostels, Inc.
132 Spring St.
New York, NY 10012

Bicycle Warehouse

Whether you need an entire wheel or the smallest nut, whether you are looking for a whole biking outfit or just a T-shirt, the Bike Warehouse has it, and, what's more, has it listed in their catalog for you to order from. It even has a special section on bike camping—all the gear and accessories you will need to carry with you when you go camping on your bike.

Send: $1.25

Ask for: catalog

Write to: Bike Warehouse
215 Main St.
New Middletown, OH 44442

Bike Oil

Keep your bike running smoothly with frequent lube jobs on the parts that get clogged and dirty. This high-quality light oil is made specifically for bicycle parts and comes in a four-ounce spout can for easy application. Always have a can with you for smooth pedaling.

Send: $1.20

Ask for: Bike Oil

Write to: American Youth Hostels, Inc.
132 Spring St.
New York, NY 10012

Biking Equipment

This 32-page color catalog displays the packs, the panniers, the carriers, the tools, the clothing, and all the accessories you will need to make your bicycle comfortable and safe. The catalog is free from the hundreds of Eclipse touring centers around the country, or available by mail for a small handling and postage fee.

Send: $1.00

Ask for: catalog

Write to: Eclipse, Inc.
P.O. Box 7370
Ann Arbor, MI 48107

Bike Parts and Accessories

If you are in need of a part for your bike or a whole new bike, this mail-order catalog is for you. A free WATS-line number lets you order over the phone. A very complete listing of parts, accessories, bikes, gear, clothing—everything you'll need.

Send: a postcard

Ask for: catalog

Write to: Bikecology
12509 Beatrice St.
P.O. Box 66-909
Los Angeles, CA 90066

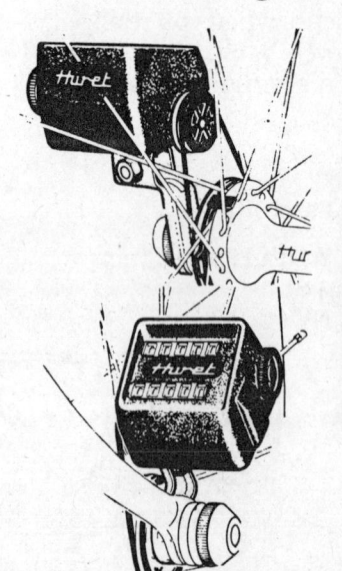

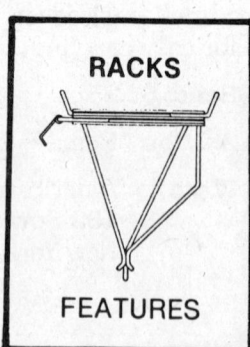

RACKS

FEATURES

Country Cycling

Country Cycling Tours has one-, two-, and three-day trips, and extended tours and vacations to places like Nova Scotia and Ireland. Most of the shorter trips are in the New York, New Jersey, and Vermont areas. This free brochure explains the various trips, the places you will stay, the types of equipment you will need. Surprise: You don't have to own a bike to go. Good, safe bikes can be rented from the group itself.

Send: a postcard

Ask for: tour guide

Write to: Country Cycling Tours
95 West 95th St.
New York, NY 10025

Bicycle Touring

Bicycle touring is the art of sightseeing on a bicycle. This 40-page booklet will tell you how to get started, how to plan a longer tour, how to get your body in shape for it. It will explain the various riding techniques to make your trip safe and comfortable, and tell you what to look for when you go shopping for gear and equipment. It also discusses the problems and solutions for getting your bike to where you want to ride—by air, bus, or rail.

Send: $2.00

Ask for: "Bicycle Touring USA"

Write to: Bicycle Touring Group of America
P.O. Box 7407, Dept. FT
Richmond, VA 23221

Changing Tires

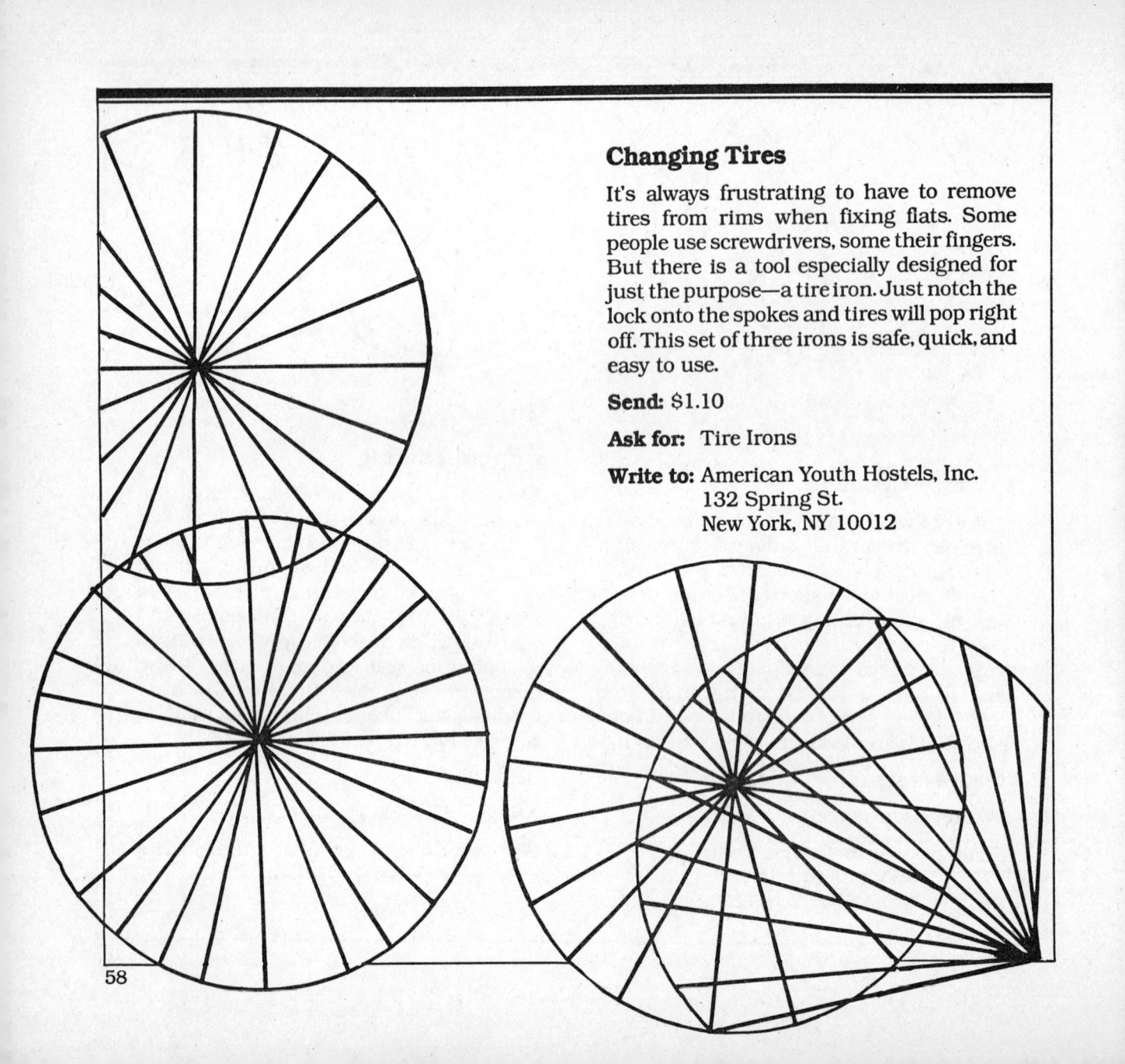

It's always frustrating to have to remove tires from rims when fixing flats. Some people use screwdrivers, some their fingers. But there is a tool especially designed for just the purpose—a tire iron. Just notch the lock onto the spokes and tires will pop right off. This set of three irons is safe, quick, and easy to use.

Send: $1.10

Ask for: Tire Irons

Write to: American Youth Hostels, Inc.
132 Spring St.
New York, NY 10012

Biking Accessories

This free catalog will show you all the many gadgets and gizmos that will make your cycling safer and more fun. It includes clothing (for day and night, all types of weather), front and back carriers, packs and bags, water bottle cages, helmets, even training devices for racers, like training weights and wind load simulators.

Send: a postcard

Ask for: cycling accessories catalog

Write to: Meyer Athletics, Inc.
P.O. Box 94454
Schaumbur, IL 60194

Cyclist's Logbook

Keep track of your long bike trips with this 42-page logbook. Easy to carry and use. Make notes for future trips and good old reminiscing when the trip is over.

Send: $1.50

Ask for: "Cyclist's Logbook"

Write to: Rhode Gear USA
P.O. Box 1087
Providence, RI 02901

Spoke Reflectors

Biking across intersections and driveways at night is safer with a brightly spinning spoke reflector on each wheel. Let approaching motorists see clearly that you got there first! Bike safely with a flashing whirl of light on each wheel.

Send: $1.75

Ask for: Spoke Reflectors

Write to: American Youth Hostels, Inc.
132 Spring St.
New York, NY 10012

West Coast Cycle Tours

If you want great cycling, beautiful scenery, merry camaraderie, and good food, send for this pamphlet about cycling tours of the West Coast. Included are trips to Death Valley, Big Sur, the Grand Tetons and Yellowstone, Glacier, the Russian River, the Napa Valley, the Colorado Rockies, the Grand Canyon, and many more. Trips are five- and six-day or weekend and three-day, some with camping, others with hotels. Choose the ones that suit you best!

Send: $1.00

Ask for: tour catalog

Write to: Backroads Bicycle Touring Co.
P.O. Box 5534F
Berkeley, CA 94705

Biking Through Vermont

Vermont bicycle touring is for adults and families with a spirit of adventure and a taste for country hospitality. These tours are carefully designed for your comfort and ease and to capitalize on the breathtaking change of seasons in Vermont. There are tours for beginners, intermediates, and advanced riders. Some tours are roundabouts over weekends, others are five-day wanderer tours from inn to inn.

Send: a postcard

Ask for: Vermont Bicycle Touring catalog

Write to: Vermont Bicycle Touring
R.D. 3
Bristol, VT 05443

Dumbbell Wrench

Every biker knows that loose parts on a bike do more than just rattle. They warn of possibly serious accidents—should an important part become dangerously loose. With a good dumbbell wrench in your tool kit, you'll be able to tighten almost any nut on your bike. This 10-in-one wrench is one of the most reliable and valuable tools you can invest in.

Send: $1.25

Ask for: dumbbell wrench

Write to: American Youth Hostels, Inc.
132 Spring St.
New York, NY 10012

Small Accessories

Rhode Gear has a new catalog of minor accessories for bikes. Included are ankle straps, rear carriers, flickstands, a cageless water bottle, and handlebar hides.

Send: a postcard

Ask for: 1982 catalog

Write to: Rhode Gear USA
P.O. Box 1087
Providence, RI 02901

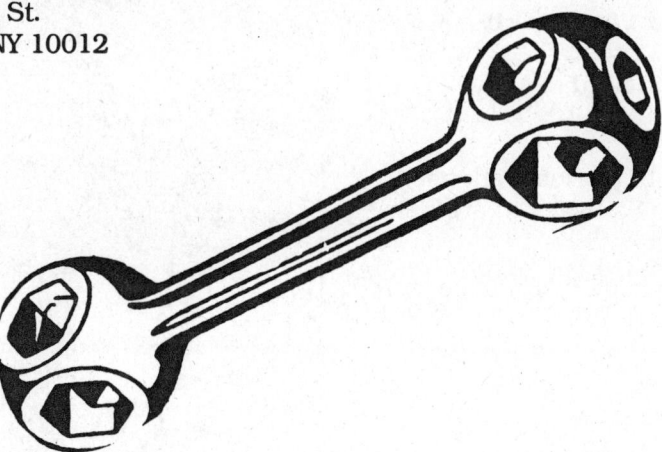

VI. Fishing and Boating

Florida Fishing

Surrounded on three sides by water, Florida is a natural for fishing. In this state there are always fish to catch! Get the facts about saltwater fishing, the laws, the licensing requirements, and the various regions of the state and what types of fish you can expect to catch in them. These two leaflets will tell you all you need to know.

Send: a postcard

Ask for: "Facts for Florida Fishermen"
"Florida Saltwater Sport Fishing Booklet"

Write to: Department of Natural Resources
Marjorie Stoneman Douglas Bldg.
3900 Commonwealth Blvd.
Tallahassee, Fl 32303

Build Your Own Boat

Why build a boat? In a nutshell—savings, quality, and personal satisfaction. Of course, you might also want to build for profit, that is, build one and sell it. This boat builder's guide lists kits, plans, supplies, hardware, and accessories for kayaks and canoes. Learn the differences in material, design, and construction...and then build your own!

Send: $2.00

Ask for: "Boat Builders' Guide"

Write to: Clark Craft Boat Co.
16 Aqua Lane
Tonawanda, NY 14150

Canoes

Canoeing down the river safely depends on many things, not the least of which is the quality of your canoe. For a look at Coleman's latest models, colors, and designs, send for this free catalog listing the various options that are now available on modern canoes. There is even one called a Scanoe—a canoe with a square stern. The catalog also lists various accessories.

Send: a postcard

Ask for: Coleman canoes catalog

Write to: The Coleman Co.
250 N. St. Francis
Wichita, KS 67201

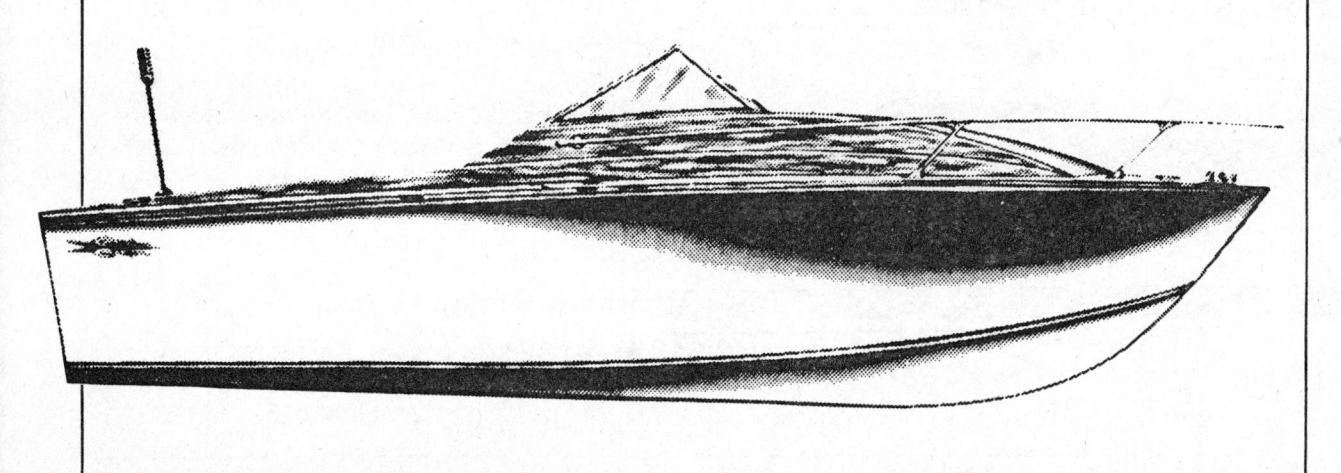

Fishing Magazine

"The Inside Line" gives you valuable information about fishing and updates you on what's going on around the world of fishing. Learn how to avoid backlashes and tie intricate knots, and find out about trout fishing in Tasmania. Write for a sample issue.

Send: 25¢

Ask for: "The Inside Line"

Write to: Cortland Line Co.
67 E. Court St.
Cortland, NY 13045

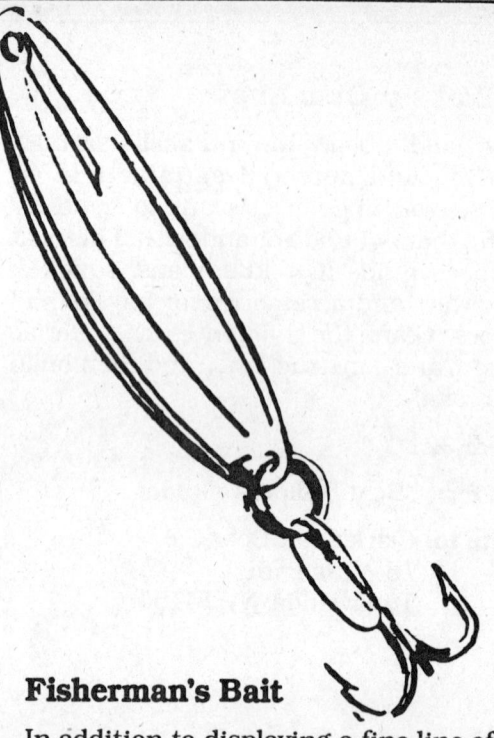

Fisherman's Bait

In addition to displaying a fine line of bait and lures, this catalog will show you the latest tanks and aerating systems to save your bait, keeping it alive and kicking until you need it.

Send: $1.00

Ask for: catalog

Write to: Marine Metal Products Co.
1222 Range Ave.
Clearwater, FL 33515

64

Fishing Techniques

This pamphlet, written by seven famous fishermen—successful fishermen—explains ways to use pork rind bait in fresh water. Learn how to catch largemouth bass, striped bass, walleye pike, smallmouth bass, northern pike, and panfish by the experts who have caught plenty.

Send: a postcard

Ask for: "How to Fish Pork Rind in Fresh Water"

Write to: Uncle Josh Bait Co.
Fort Atkinson, WI 53538

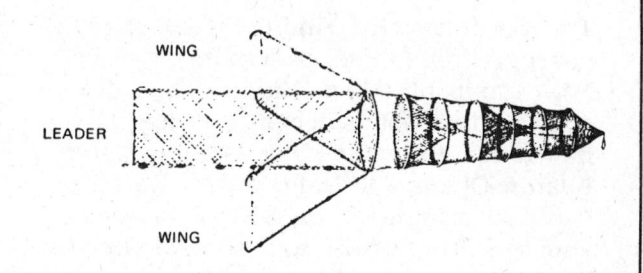

For the Serious Fisherman

This catalog will give commercial and subsistence fishermen a wide choice of nets, trawls, seines, and lines that you may want to have to improve your catch. This catalog also shows the proper sequence for launching a trawl from a small boat and gives some practical tips on trawling. Included are price lists and order forms.

Send: $2.00

Ask for: Supplies for Commercial and Subsistence Fishermen catalog

Write to: Sea Isle Net Co., Inc.
129 Druid Oaks Lane
P.O. Box 570
St. Simons Island, GA 31522

Canoeing in New England

The Saco and the Androscoggin rivers, flowing through the wilderness areas of New Hampshire and Maine, offer ideal opportunities for canoeing and learning how to ride the white waters bound for the Atlantic Ocean. This leaflet will give you the lowdown on rentals, camping, equipment shops, rafting trips, and the Northern Waters Whitewater School, which teaches the skills you need to enjoy the excitement of white-water canoeing.

Send: a postcard

Ask for: brochure

Write to: Saco Bound/Northern Waters
P.O. Box 113
Center Conway, NH 03813

Fly Strip on Marabou Jig

Little Vee on 00 Mepps Spinner

Fishing Bait

As Uncle Josh puts it, his bait is meant to create the illusion that "there's something alive around here and it's probably good to eat." So catch it. That's not hard to do with Uncle Josh bait. Pork rind baits, specially scented baits, and artificial lures will help you snag those bass, catfish, salmon, and trout for which they were made. This brochure will let you survey Uncle Josh baits and lures and read about the different ways they may be used.

Send: 25¢

Ask for: "A Natural Underwater"

Write to: Uncle Josh Bait Co.
Fort Atkinson, WI 53538

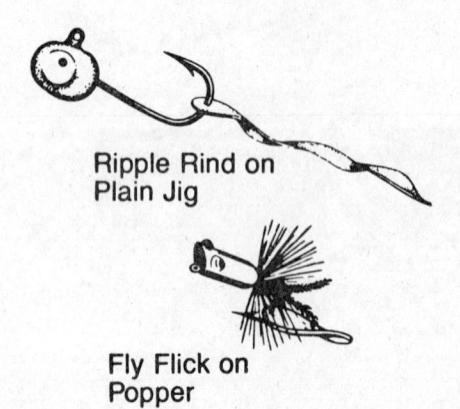

Ripple Rind on Plain Jig

Fly Flick on Popper

Scientific Anglers

Besides an up-to-date listing of their equipment, this catalog contains something special. It's called "The Right Fly Line for You." Improve your fishing with the proper fly-line selection. This guide will explain how.

Send: 50¢

Ask for: catalog

Write to: Scientific Anglers/3M Co.
3M Center, Bldg. 223-3S
Dept. A-HB1
St. Paul, MN 55101

Fishing Bait

Twin Lakes Bait Co. supplies you with everything but the fish. The new 1982 catalog is bigger than ever and includes a section on everything you need to make your own lures. Most of the bait sold for catfish will have a money-back guarantee if you don't catch any fish with it. The new secret blend of ingredients to flavor this catfish bait will drive those catfish wild!

Send: $1.00

Ask for: 1982 bait catalog

Write to: Twin Lakes Bait Co.
P.O. Box 56
Rineyville, KY 40162

Building a Sailboat

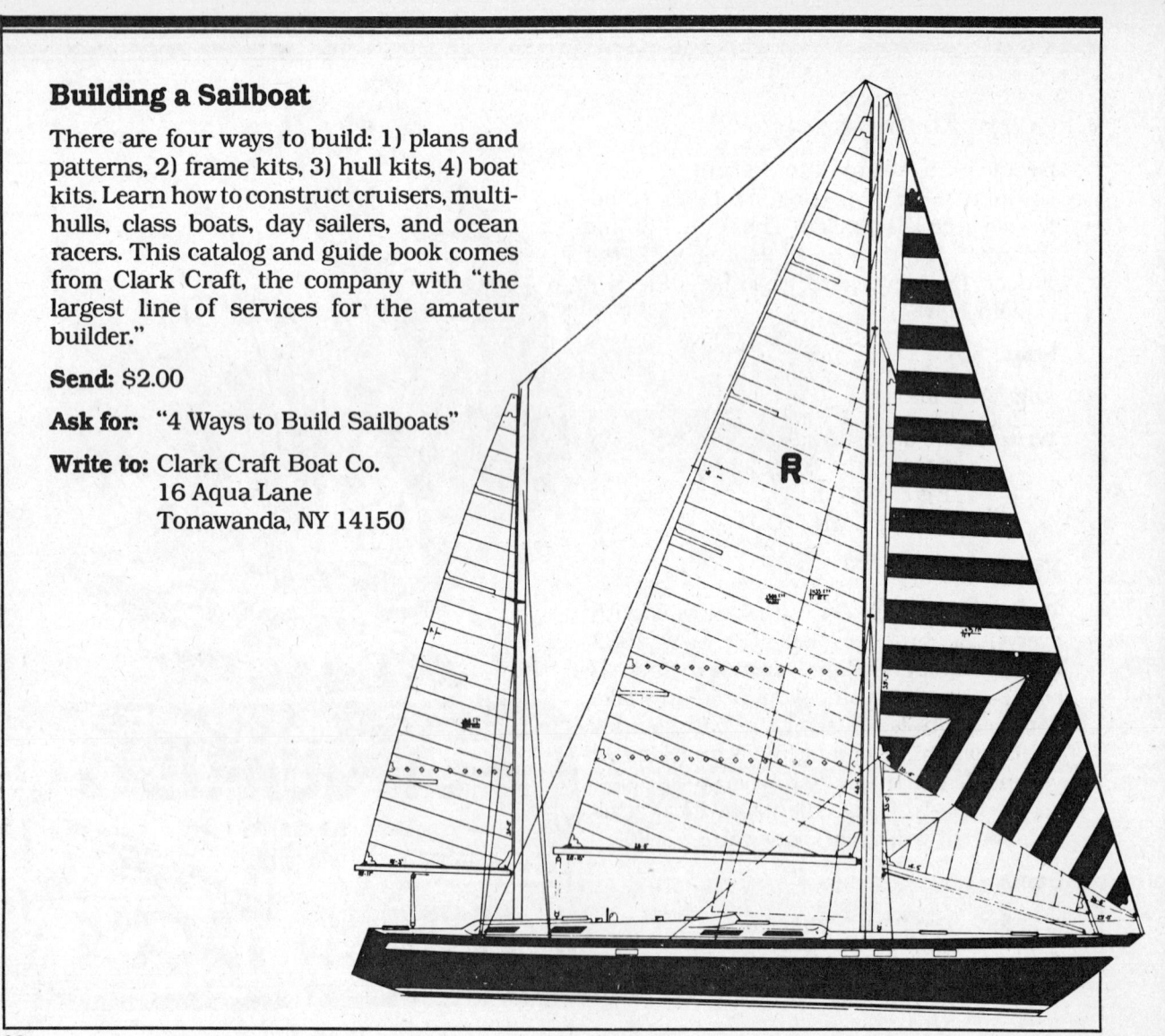

There are four ways to build: 1) plans and patterns, 2) frame kits, 3) hull kits, 4) boat kits. Learn how to construct cruisers, multi-hulls, class boats, day sailers, and ocean racers. This catalog and guide book comes from Clark Craft, the company with "the largest line of services for the amateur builder."

Send: $2.00

Ask for: "4 Ways to Build Sailboats"

Write to: Clark Craft Boat Co.
16 Aqua Lane
Tonawanda, NY 14150

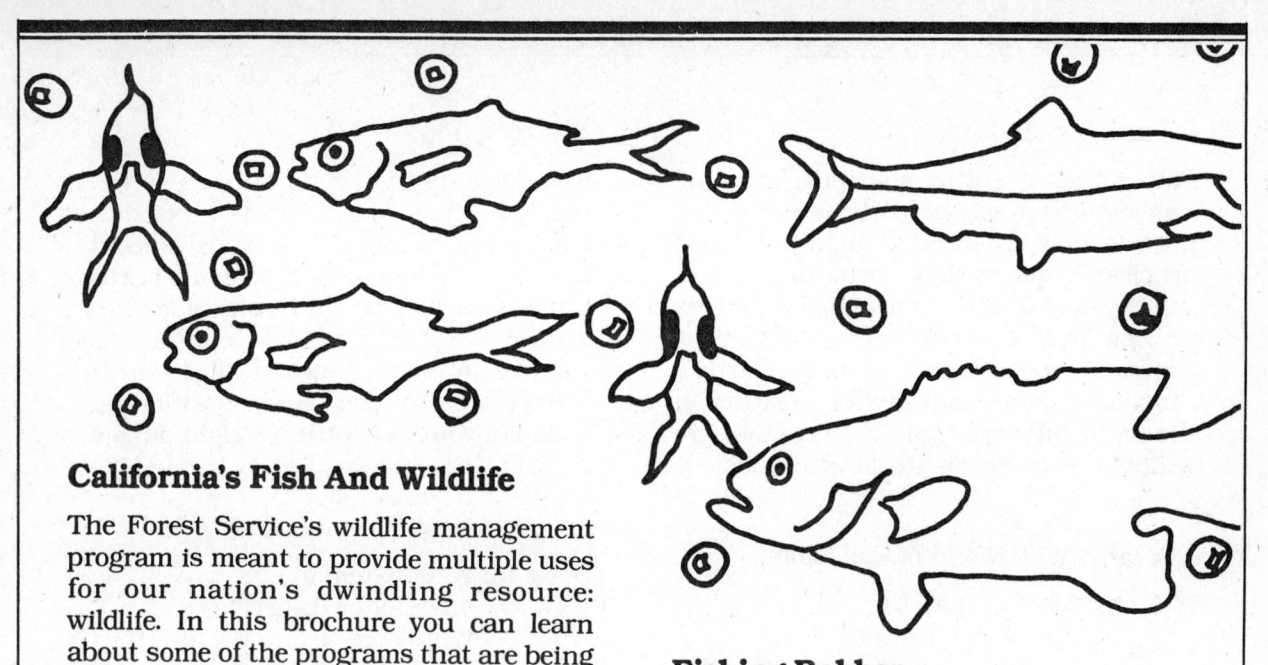

California's Fish And Wildlife

The Forest Service's wildlife management program is meant to provide multiple uses for our nation's dwindling resource: wildlife. In this brochure you can learn about some of the programs that are being carried out in California. The endangered-species program is of particular interest, a program protecting the huge condor and the tiny unarmored threespine stickleback (a fish).

Send: a postcard

Ask for: "Fish and Wildlife in the National Forests in California"

Write to: Office of Information
Pacific Southwest Region
USDA–Forest Service
630 Sansome St.
San Francisco, CA 94111

Fishing Bobber

A sneaky bobber for sneaky biters! This fishing bobber just might be the most sensitive bobber ever made. It can be installed on plain wire, snap-on wire, and snap-on nylon. Good for both summer and winter tight-line fishing. Attaches to your fishing rod easily, in seconds.

Send: $1.00

Ask for: Sneaky Bobber

Write to: Magic Match Patch Co.
4365 Letart
Drayton Plains, MI 48020

Canoeing Annual

For canoeing enthusiasts, this annual publication from the Coleman Co. will provide interesting and thought-provoking articles to inform you about the care of canoes, how to use them, and suggestions on new places to go for your next trips. Practical articles on finances, starting canoeing businesses, and what to expect on the many different types of rivers that are suitable for canoeing are also included.

Send: $1.50

Ask for: "Wide World of Canoeing"

Write to: The Coleman Co.
250 N. St. Francis
Wichita, KS 67201

Fishing Tips

Knowledge is the key to success—even at the old fishin' hole. Here is a booklet of fishing tips to give you some new ideas on how you can use sinkers to catch more fish. Sinkers used to be old hunks of lead that you tied onto your line. Now newly designed sinkers do more than just sink. You can actually control the depth, position, and action of your bait with the right sinker.

Send: $1.00

Ask for: "Fishin' Sinker Tips"

Write to: Water Gremlin Co.
4370 Otter Lake Rd.
White Bear Lake, MN 55110

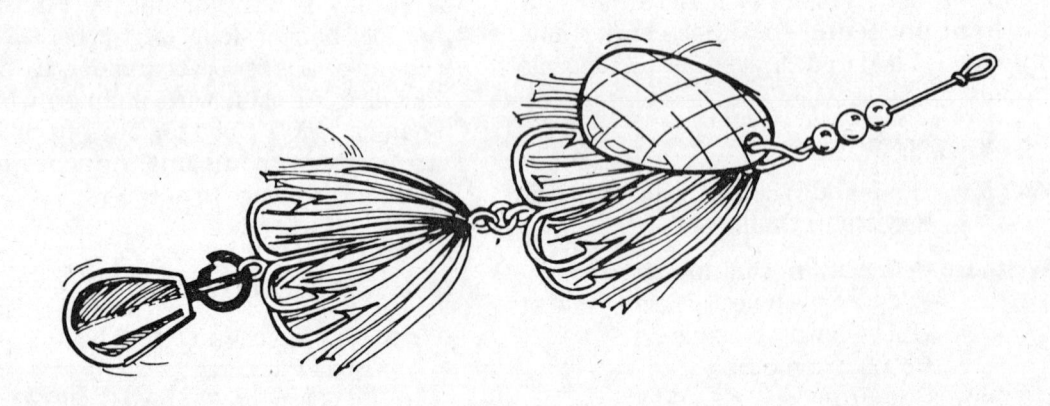

Homemade Power Boats

This catalog covers a wide range of designs to satisfy the race enthusiast, the fisherman, and the pleasure boater. Included are cruisers, hydros, and runabouts, listed with basic specifications, prices, photos, and supplementary sketches. There are 46 pages of boats, boats, and more boats.

Send: $2.00

Ask for: "4 Ways to Build Power Boats"

Write to: Clark Craft Boat Co.
16 Aqua Lane
Tonawanda, NY 14150

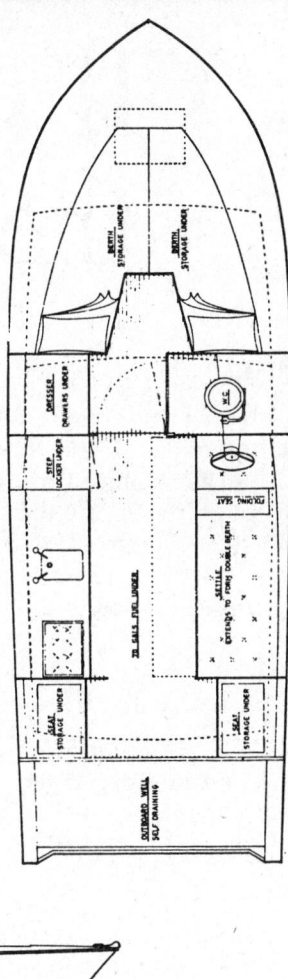

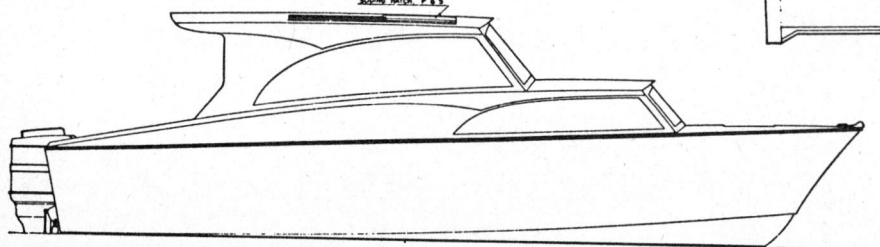

VII. Coping with the Outdoors

Repair Stick

This melt-and-patch repair stick will fix breaks, rips, or punctures with hot adhesive. It sticks to almost any clean, dry surface except lightweight vinyl. You'll find a thousand different uses for this handy repair kit in a stick. Lightweight, too, for easy backpacking: .05 lbs.

Send: $1.50

Ask for: Melt and Patch Repair Stick (No. 56)

Write to: Moor and Mountain
63 Park St.
Andover, MA 01810

Plastic Soap Dish

This extremely lightweight soap dish will hold one regular-size bar of your favorite soap for washing in the woods. Soap up, close your eyes, and you can almost imagine you're in the comfort of your own bathroom. Size: ¾″ by 4″ by 2½″. Weight: 1.25 ounces.

Send: 75¢

Ask for: Plastic Soap Dish

Write to: American Youth Hostels, Inc.
132 Spring St.
New York, NY 10012

Waterproofing Boots

Anyone who has hiked through snow or rain knows the importance of good waterproofing. If you have an older pair of boots or a new pair that are not very water-resistant, you can seal them yourself with this wax-base boot preservative with silicone added. This waterproofer tends not to soften leather.

Send: $2.00

Ask for: Sno Seal (No. 35-0066)

Write to: Eastern Mountain Sports
Vose Farm Rd.
Peterborough, NH 03458

Candles

These "Pink Ladies" are dripless and smokeless. Good for lanterns or just on their own when you need a light. They will burn up to six hours. Size: ¾" by 5".

Send: 15¢ each

Ask for: Candles (No. 507)

Write to: Moor and Mountain
63 Park St.
Andover, MA 01810

Bites and Stings

They always getcha! No matter what you do, there will always be flying and crawling critters to make your hike unpleasant. Learn about repellents, clothing, habitats, and—most of all—how to avoid attracting bugs with perfumes, deodorants, and certain colors. This pamphlet covers mosquitoes, ants, blackflies, punkies, deerflies, and bees.

Send: 20¢

Ask for: "Coping with Biting Trail Bugs of the Northeast"

Write to: Adirondack Mountain Club, Inc.
172 Ridge St.
Glens Falls, NY 12801

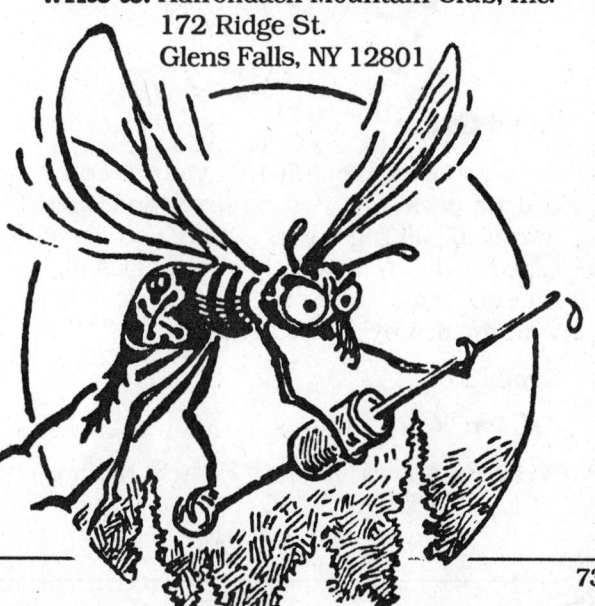

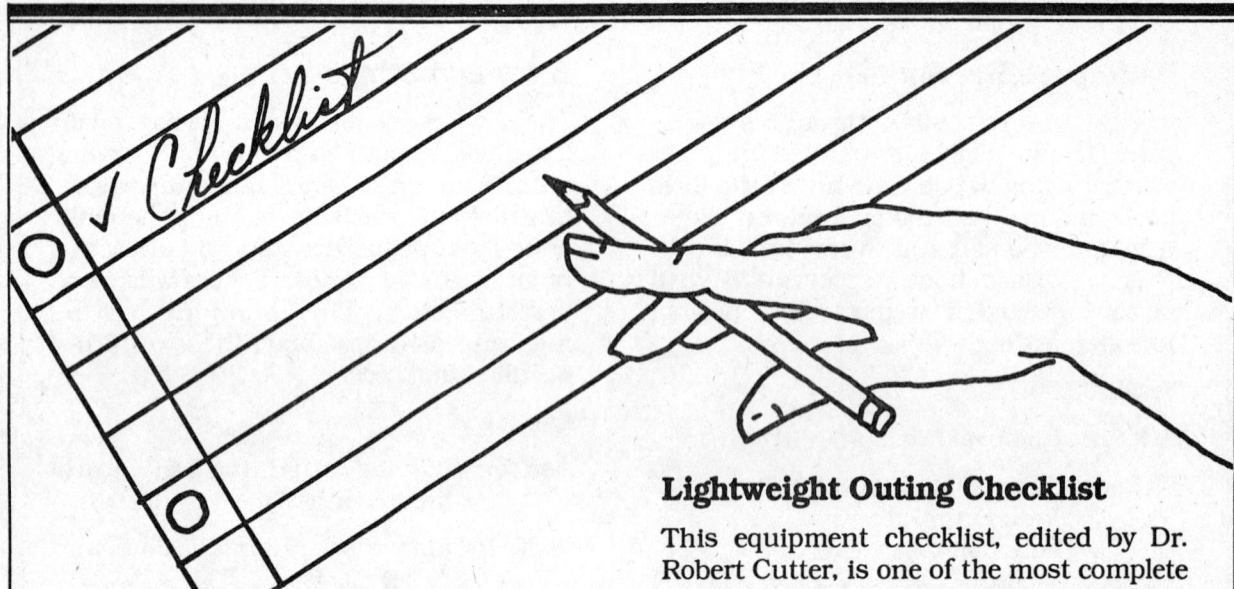

Cord Grips

Have you ever thought that your sleeping bag or pack was tied securely and then found it falling apart when you least expected it to? Now tie your bundles and hike on, knowing they are securely fastened with molded nylon cord grips.

Send: 60¢

Ask for: Cord Grips

Write to: American Youth Hostels, Inc.
132 Spring St.
New York, NY 10012

Lightweight Outing Checklist

This equipment checklist, edited by Dr. Robert Cutter, is one of the most complete lists of its type, including excellent descriptions of the most common items you will want to take with you. One of the things you'll learn if you are a first-timer is that you don't have to take everything you might need. And you shouldn't! On the back of this list is a good directory of addresses of the major outdoor equipment suppliers.

Send: 10¢

Ask for: "Lightweight Equipment Checklist"

Write to: Sierra Club
Information Services
530 Bush St.
San Francisco, CA 94108

Dr. Bonner's Castile Peppermint Soap

This reliable brand-name soap is made of pure, biodegradable ingredients and comes in an unbreakable plastic bottle with flip top. The four-ounce size is handy for camping and hiking.

Send: $1.00

Ask for: Dr. Bonner's Castile Peppermint Soap

Write to: American Youth Hostels, Inc.
132 Spring St.
New York, NY 10012

Wilderness Tips

There are four components to every camping trip: preparation, the trail, the campsite, and the return to civilization. This pamphlet will give you general guidelines for each part of your trip. You'll also learn what to do and what not to do should you get lost.

Send: 20¢

Ask for: "Wilderness Tips"

Write to: Adirondack Mountain Club, Inc.
172 Ridge St.
Glens Falls, NY 12801

Camping and Picnicking Inventory

Here is a 13-page itemized list of the essential supplies, food, clothing, and equipment you will need on your next outing into the wilderness. In addition to the checklists, 22 hints and tips on such wide-ranging topics as mosquito netting, firearms, and portable toilets make this inventory ideal for family adventures.

Send: $2.00

Ask for: "The Compleat Camper"

Write to: Perry Pat Productions
P.O. Box 174
Jacksonville, TX 75766

Off-Hand Towelette

When you need a quick cleanup away from lavatory facilities, a fast wipe with a tingly citrus-scented towelette is just what you need. These convenient cleansers can handle dirt, ink, and other smudges—even bike-chain grease. Each bag contains 16 towelettes for instant cleanups.

Send: 80¢

Ask for: Off-Hand Towelette

Write to: American Youth Hostels, Inc.
132 Spring St.
New York, NY 10012

Summer Backpacking

For the summer backpacker, here is a great checklist of personal and common equipment you will need. Also included are preplanning tips, general information about gear and clothing, and safety rules for the trail and around the campfire.

Send: 20¢

Ask for: "For the Summer Backpacker"

Write to: Adirondack Mountain Club, Inc.
172 Ridge St.
Glens Falls, NY 12801

Hypothermia

If your body loses more heat than it can produce, your body's inner core temperature begins to drop. If not halted, death follows within two hours. Don't take chances by camping or hiking in the winter cold without knowing about hypothermia and how to combat it.

Send: 20¢

Ask for: "Hypothermia, A Killer Companion"

Write to: Adirondack Mountain Club, Inc.
172 Ridge St.
Glens Falls, NY 12801

"Baby" Carabiner

These small 60-mm. carabiners are too weak for hefty climbing but convenient for other outdoor purposes where the free play of rope is needed, as in hoisting or lifting bundles off the ground.

Send: $1.35

Ask for: Baby Carabiner

Write to: American Youth Hostels, Inc.
132 Spring St.
New York, NY 10012

Sportsman's Soap

You don't have to worry about polluting the environment when you soap up in the outdoors with sportsman's soap made of a mild, biodegradable coconut oil. A concentrated liquid in two leakproof tubes, this cleanser will give you over 50 or more washings per tube. Each order contains one card of two 21.3-gram tubes.

Send: $1.30

Ask for: Sportsman's Soap

Write to: American Youth Hostels, Inc.
132 Spring St.
New York, NY 10012

Grizzlies

The strongest and most ferocious mammal in North America, the grizzly bear, is someone you should know something about if you intend to visit its natural habitat in Idaho, Wyoming, or Montana. Become familiar with its habits and tendencies. Learn what to do and not to do should you meet one.

Send: a postcard

Ask for: "Grizzly Grizzly Grizzly"

Write to: National Park Service
P.O. Box 168
Yellowstone National Park
WY 82190

Ditty Bag

Keep all your toilet articles collected in one easy-to-reach place as outdoors people have done for generations—in an authentic ditty bag. Rubberized to keep liquids from leaking onto clothing and other articles, this handy green bag with drawstring is 10" by 12". Don't leave your tent without one!

Send: $1.10

Ask for: Ditty Bag

Write to: American Youth Hostels, Inc.
132 Spring St.
New York, NY 10012

Bears

Bears are interesting but dangerous animals. They look cuddly and remind us of childhood stuffed animals, but beware. They are not as friendly as Smokey. Here is a pamphlet that will give you the "bear facts" about how to encounter and survive your adventures with these woodland creatures.

Send: 20¢

Ask for: "The Bear Facts"

Write to: Adirondack Mountain Club, Inc.
172 Ridge St.
Glens Falls, NY 12801

Matchbox

If you don't forget them, you usually get them wet. Well, this little box won't prevent you from forgetting them, but it will certainly keep them dry. Made of sturdy high-impact styrene with a waterproof screw top. A striking flint is built into the base.

Send: 70¢

Ask for: Waterproof Matchbox (No. 409)

Write to: Moor and Mountain
63 Park St.
Andover, MA 01810

Band Saw

You can't always carry hatchets and axes with you when you need to travel light. But you can still saw small logs with this two-ounce, 18" band saw. It's made of hardened steel with finger rings at each end. You and a partner can cut your logs to size for evening campfires. One ring is removable for use as a keyhole saw.

Send: $1.95

Ask for: Band Saw

Write to: American Youth Hostels, Inc.
132 Spring St.
New York, NY 10012

"Permanent" Match

With this match you won't have to worry about losing your others to rivers, rainstorms, or damp air. This one always strikes. Just put lighter fluid in the reservoir. Unscrew this metal match and strike it against flint that comes with it. The wick will light and produce a strong, long-lasting flame. Size: 1¾" by 1⅛" by ⅜". Weight: .5 ounce.

Send: $2.00

Ask for: Permanent Match (No. 64-6620)

Write to: Eastern Mountain Sports
Vose Farm Rd.
Peterborough, NH 03458

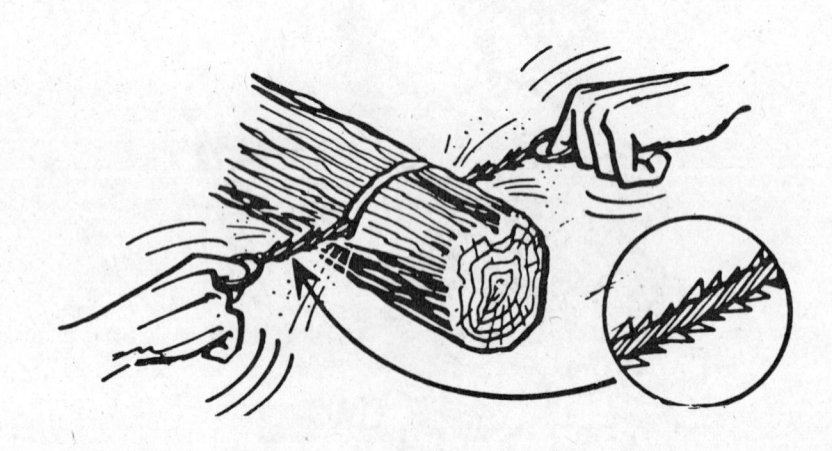

Winter Mountaineers

You see them in the summer with their snowy peaks, and you know that you have to be in them in winter—mountains! What are they like in the dead of winter? For some people the experience is hard to resist. If you've never gone mountaineering in the winter, this pamphlet is for you. Complete with checklist, safety rules, general tips, and hints to make your winter adventure safe and fun.

Send: 20¢

Ask for: "For the Winter Mountaineer"

Write to: Adirondack Mountain Club, Inc.
172 Ridge St.
Glens Falls, NY 12801

Key Ring

Don't lose your car and house keys on the trail or in the river during your weekend jaunts into the countryside. Attach them to this key ring with a leather holder that straps onto your belt or belt loop.

Send: 45¢

Ask for: Key Ring

Write to: American Youth Hostels, Inc.
132 Spring St.
New York, NY 10012

Writing in the Rain

Have you ever caught yourself in a pouring rain just when you thought you'd sketch the view from the mountain? Do snowflakes land on your mileage log and blur out your last entry? Now you can write in any weather, no matter how wet. Rain Notes are waterproof pages of specially treated paper that lets you write with a regular lead pencil or a Space pen even underwater. Each pad of 50 sheets is 3¼ by 5" and ruled on one side.

Send: $1.95

Ask for: Rain Notes (No. 0510)

Write to: Early Winters, Ltd.
110 Prefontaine Place South
Seattle, WA 98104

Nylon Cord

Don't get ready to stretch a line for your tarp or washing and find out that you are just a few feet short of the tree. Keep plenty of cording with you when you venture into the wilderness. This strong nylon cord can withstand a 650-lb. test.

Send: $1.20 (for 50 feet)

Ask for: Nylon Cord

Write to: American Youth Hostels, Inc.
132 Spring St.
New York, NY 10012

Folding Scissors

You won't have to worry about cutting yourself when you reach in your stuff sack for this pair of scissors. The blades ingeniously fold into the handles, collapsing into an overall length of 3". Take them fishing, hiking, camping, or wherever you anticipate needing emergency first-aid supplies. The handles are chrome-plated and the blades are surgical steel.

Send: $1.95

Ask for: Folding Scissors (No. 593)

Write to: Moor and Mountain
63 Park St.
Andover, MA 01810

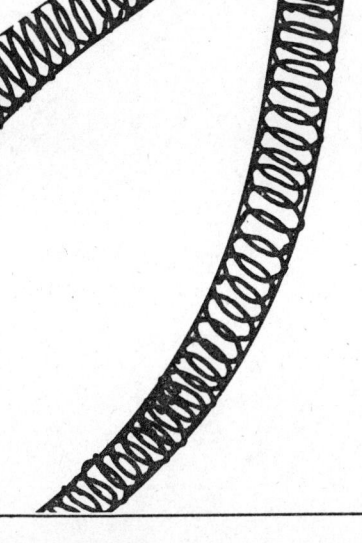

Zip Bags

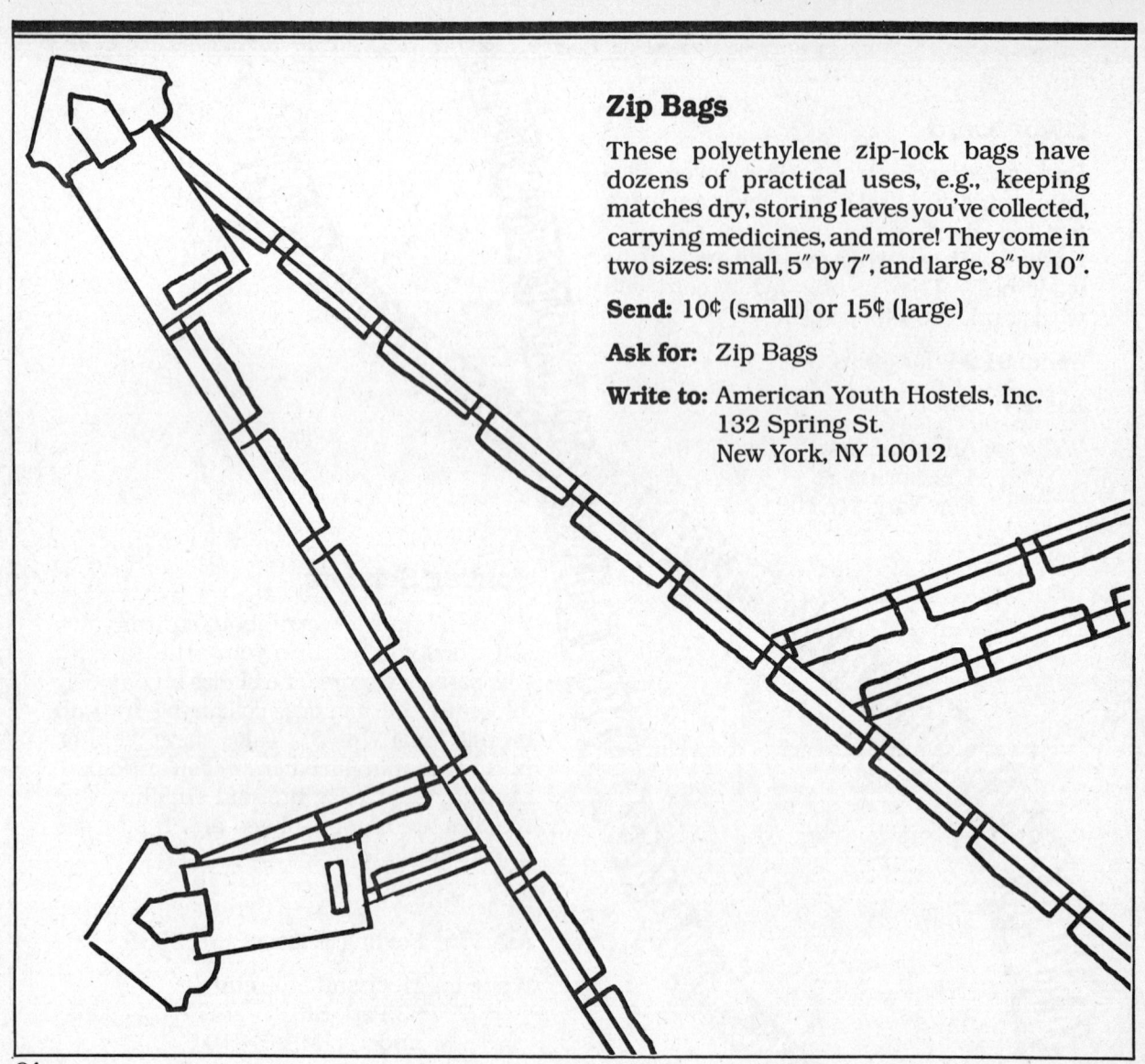

These polyethylene zip-lock bags have dozens of practical uses, e.g., keeping matches dry, storing leaves you've collected, carrying medicines, and more! They come in two sizes: small, 5" by 7", and large, 8" by 10".

Send: 10¢ (small) or 15¢ (large)

Ask for: Zip Bags

Write to: American Youth Hostels, Inc.
132 Spring St.
New York, NY 10012

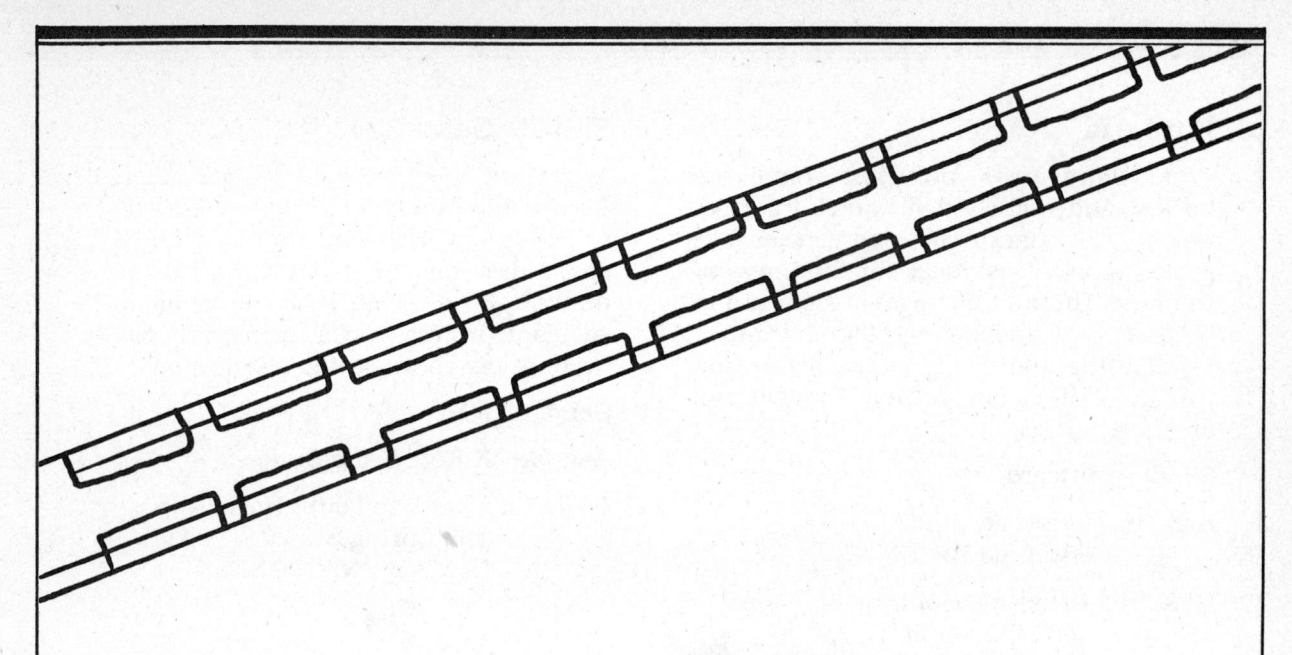

Fire Ribbon

Smear this paste onto wet wood and light it for a long-lasting flame. This fire ribbon can also be used as a stove primer. Each tube weighs five ounces.

Send: $2.00

Ask for: Fire Ribbon (No. 64-6521)

Write to: Eastern Mountain Sports
Vose Farm Rd.
Peterborough, NH 03458

Repair Tape

With more and more outdoor items being made of nylon these days, it becomes imperative to carry nylon repair tape in your first-aid or emergency kit. These tapes are adhesive-backed fabrics that come in assorted colors. Catch those small tears and rips before you can crawl through them!

Send: $1.30

Ask for: Repair Tape

Write to: American Youth Hostels, Inc.
132 Spring St.
New York, NY 10012

First Aid

From Johnson & Johnson come this booklet and wall chart for quick information on those unexpected emergencies. The pocket booklet is ideal for hiking and camping. There are 64 pages of medical and first-aid facts and step-by-step procedures for treating the common accidents and injuries that can happen anywhere, anytime.

Send: a postcard

Ask for: "First-Aid Guide"
"First-Aid Facts"

Write to: Johnson & Johnson
Consumer Affairs
New Brunswick, NJ 08903

K-Kote Seam Sealer

Nylon and other synthetic fabrics are great for keeping rain and river water out, except in the seams, where the waterproofing can sometimes fail. Stay dry with this two-ounce tube of seam sealer. Give all your seams a protective coat and catch minor leaks before they become major ones.

Send: $1.99

Ask for: K-Kote Seam Sealer

Write to: American Youth Hostels, Inc.
132 Spring St.
New York, NY 10012

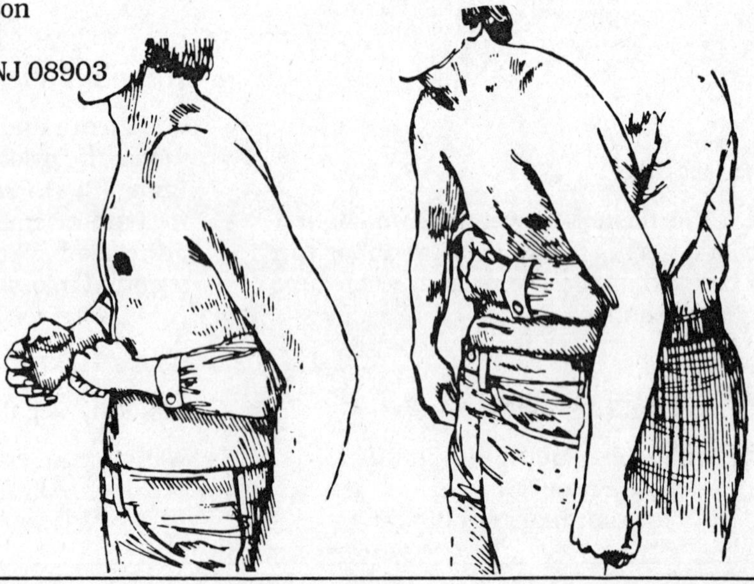

Cutting Firewood in California

Here is a brochure that will give you the basic things to consider before you chop firewood in California's national forests. The basic equipment includes a chainsaw, proper clothing, fire extinguisher, and shovel. Be sure you know the seasonal limits lest you deplete an area. Learn where the acceptable areas are for cutting. Also included is a "safety first" list.

Send: a postcard

Ask for: "Cutting Firewood in the National Forests in California"

Write to: Office of Information
Pacific Southwest Region
USDA-Forest Service
630 Sansome St.
San Francisco, CA 94111

Emergency Medical Equipment

You should always carry emergency medical equipment conveniently packed in one place for easy access. Early Winters, Ltd., makes the following three items available individually: sterile gauze compress, wire splint, and Carlisle field dressing. Keep a supply for your first-aid kit.

Send: $1.99

Ask for: Sterile Gauze Compress (No. 6809)

Send: $1.99

Ask for: Wire Splint (No. 6808)

Send: $1.75

Ask for: Carlisle Field Dressing (No. 6806)

Write to: Early Winters, Ltd.
110 Prefontaine Place South
Seattle, WA 98104

Moleskin

Every active person suffers occasionally from sore feet. Pinching, rubbing, and blisters can ruin an evening after hard-played sporting activities. Keep moleskin in your pocket, pack, or locker and suffer no more.

Send: $1.50

Ask for: Moleskin

Write to: American Youth Hostels, Inc.
132 Spring St.
New York, NY 10012

Insect Repellent

Shoo flies and mosquitoes away with Cutter Cream Repellent. It comes in a one-ounce plastic bottle—a light and efficient way to carry insect repellent on the trail. You can rely on this old proven formula.

Send: $1.80

Ask for: Cutter Cream Repellent (No. 548)

Write to: Moor and Mountain
63 Park St.
Andover, MA 01810

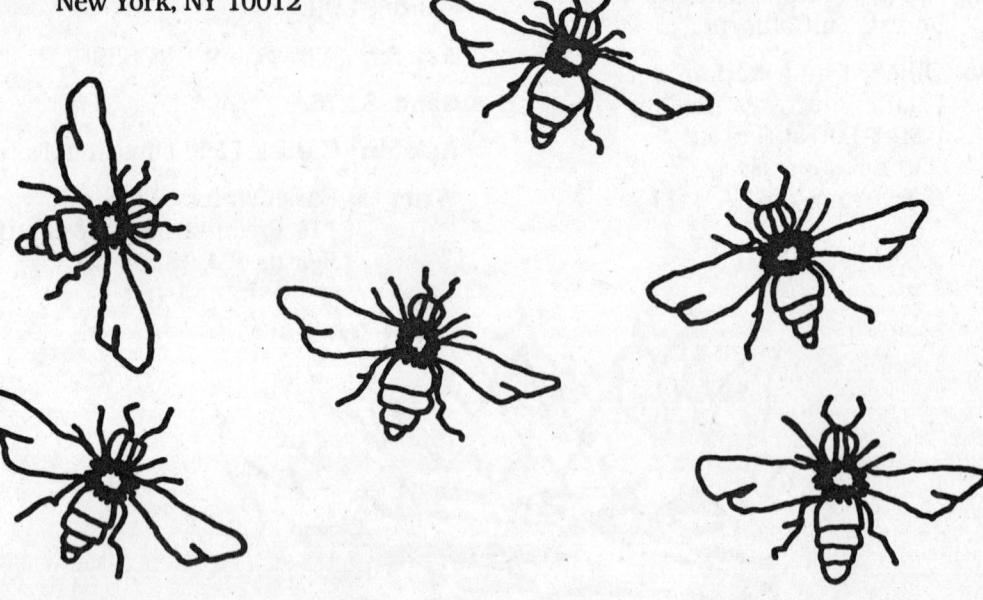

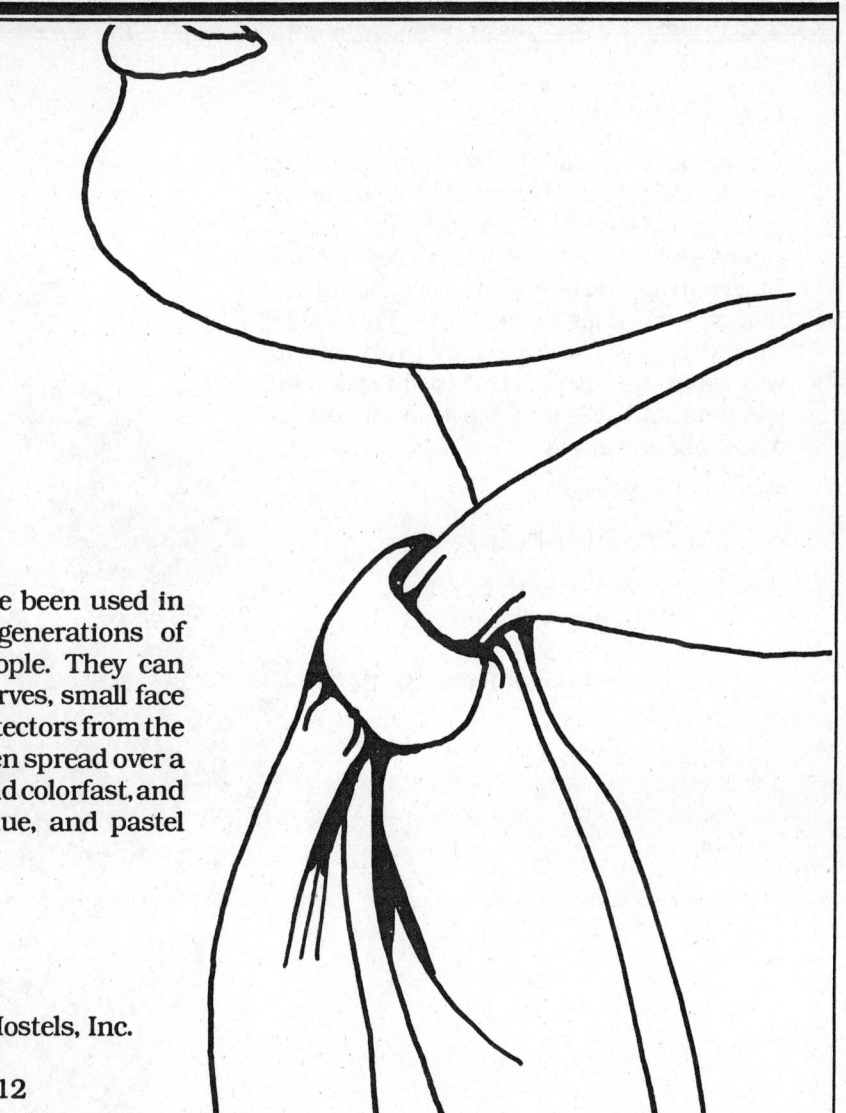

Bandannas

Traditional bandannas have been used in many different ways by generations of pioneers and outdoors people. They can serve as handkerchiefs, scarves, small face cloths for washing, neck protectors from the sun, and as water filters when spread over a pot. They are 100% cotton and colorfast, and come in dark red, dark blue, and pastel shades.

Send: 85¢ (dark colors)
$1.10 (pastel shades)

Ask for: Bandannas

Write to: American Youth Hostels, Inc.
132 Spring St.
New York, NY 10012

Black Bears!

The behavior of black bears toward people is not completely predictable. If you are going to be in their natural habitat in the north woods during seasons when they are not hibernating, you ought to know about their habits, their likes and dislikes. This leaflet from Voyageurs National Park in Minnesota will give handy advice to hikers and campers and tell you what to do if you see one—a bear, that is.

Send: a postcard

Ask for: "Caution: Bears"

Write to: National Park Service
Voyageurs National Park
P.O. Box 50
International Falls, MN 56649

Sporting Injuries

Leisure-time and professional athletes have at least one thing in common—they all get occasional injuries. This 26-page booklet covers treatment for a host of athletic injuries, such as sore muscles, bruises, blisters, athlete's foot, jock itch, shin splints, insect bites, tennis elbow, sunburn, nosebleed, and more. With this guidebook and some basic first-aid items, you can give your minor injury the same treatment given by athletic trainers.

Send: 50¢

Ask for: "Sports Injury Care"

Write to: Cramer Products, Inc.
P.O. Box 1001
Gardner, KS 66030

Small Stuff Sack

All those little odds and ends that you keep wedging into pockets and corners in your knapsack can now be kept together in a small stuff sack. Ideal for keys, pens, watches, compass, whatever, these 8"-by 9" bags come in red and blue. They are water-repellent nylon with cord lock.

Send: $1.69

Ask for: Small Stuff Sack

Write to: American Youth Hostels, Inc.
132 Spring St.
New York, NY 10012

Filtered Fuel Funnel

A lot of stoves clog up because of dirty fuel. This is easily avoided with a fuel funnel to filter out the debris that can so easily fall into fuel. This funnel from Coleman virtually eliminates dirty fuel to help ensure peak operating efficiency. It measures 2¾" by 3¼" overall and weighs two ounces.

Send: $2.00

Ask for: Coleman Filter Funnel (No. 64-6802)

Write to: Eastern Mountain Sports
Vose Farm Rd.
Peterborough, NH 03458

Foot Protection

These insoles are made of polyurethane foam and laminated to wool to provide excellent insulation. They are highly absorbent and fit into any boot, moccasin, or shoe. Add comfort to your next hike without buying new boots!

Send: $1.75

Ask for: Aircel Insoles (No. 674)

Write to: Moor and Mountain
63 Park St.
Andover, MA 01810

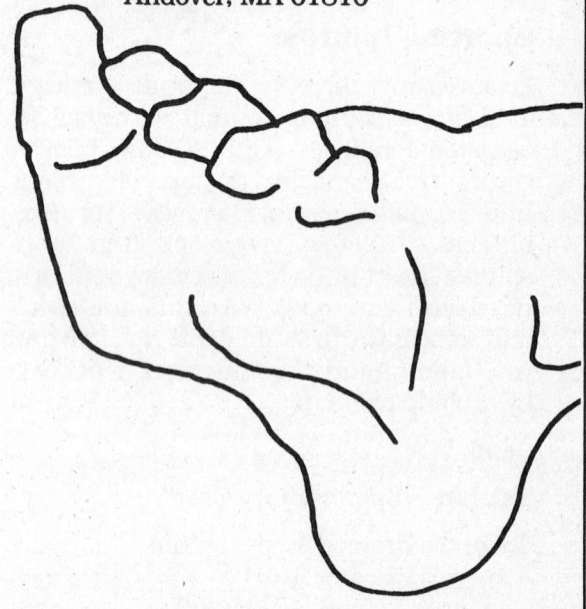

Emergency Ice

For sprains, insect bites, toothaches, and nosebleeds, use instant ice to reduce swelling, or get relief from pain in just seconds. Weighing only 4.5 ounces, this handy pack needs only a hard slap to activate it and turn it into a cold compress. Carry one on hikes and camping trips for those emergencies when an ice-cold compress is a must!

Send: $1.00

Ask for: Cutter Instant Ice (No. 67-1495)

Write to: Eastern Mountain Sports
Vose Farm Rd.
Peterborough, NH 03458

Hurricane Matches

Starting a fire in wet or windy weather is not only irritating but can lead to defeat and ruin the best-planned barbecue or campfire. What you need are windproof, waterproof matches that will give you a sure light under any weather conditions. Each order consists of three boxes, with 25 matches per box. You won't strike out with hurricane matches!

Send: $1.00

Ask for: Hurricane Matches

Write to: American Youth Hostels, Inc.
132 Spring St.
New York, NY 10012

A Trail Trowel

This plastic trowel is tough and weighs less than one pound. At 12" in length with a 6"-by-2" blade, this little digger can easily be taken on a backpacking trip.

Send: 75¢

Ask for: The Right Digger (No. 528)

Write to: Moor and Mountain
63 Park St.
Andover, MA 01810

Match Container

This match container can be fastened to your belt or pack strap with its nifty carrying ring. A tight gasket, made of sturdy metal, it is waterproof, weighs only one ounce, and has a permanent striking surface. Keep your matches dry so they don't fail you when you need them most.

Send: $1.00

Ask for: Rugged Match Container (No. 64-6547)

Write to: Eastern Mountain Sports
Vose Farm Rd.
Peterborough, NH 03458

Combination Spanner

No tool kit is quite complete without an all-purpose wrench like this combination spanner. Especially good for three-speeds, it will make your repair jobs easier and quicker so you can have more time to spend pedaling and less time repairing.

Send: $1.25

Ask for: Combination Spanner

Write to: American Youth Hostels, Inc.
132 Spring St.
New York, NY 10012

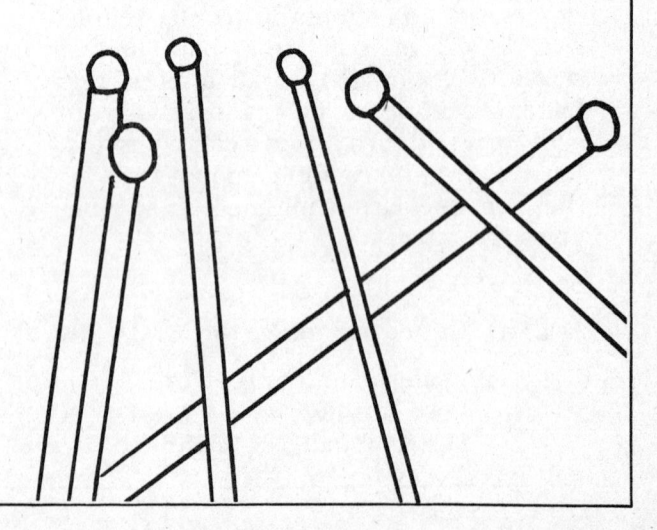

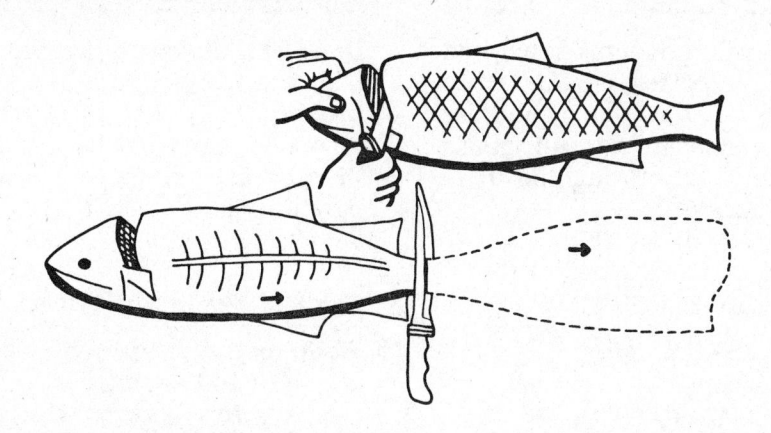

Knife Care

This 16-page booklet on the care and use of knives will teach you how handle your own knife with the finesse of a professional. The knife, one of man's oldest tools, does not need to be a source of danger. Here you will learn how to clean, sharpen, and use your Buck knife for such processes as deer dressing and filleting fish. Included is a list of dos and don'ts about knives and a price list of Buck knives.

Send: a postcard

Ask for: "Knife Know-How"

Write to: Buck Knives
P.O. Box 1267
El Cajon, CA 92022

Poly Bottles

These bottles are wide-mouthed, rigid, and made of high-density polyethylene. They are easier to clean and less likely to absorb bacteria than conventional poly bottles. Get an assortment for the various liquids you want to take with you on your outdoor adventures.

Send: 89¢ (¼ pint)

Ask for: Nalgene Poly Bottle (No. 64-0805)

Write to: Eastern Mountain Sports
Vose Farm Rd.
Peterborough, NH 03458

Eyeglasses Slip?

This elastic band with grippers on each end can be attached to eyeglasses to keep them securely in place when you enjoy outdoor activities. Comfortable and safe, this guard will take the worry out of roughing it for those who wear glasses.

Send: $1.50

Ask for: Glass Gard (No. 594)

Write to: Moor and Mountain
63 Park St.
Andover, MA 01810

Toothbrush Holder

Don't let the sticky, leaky items in your toilet bag ruin your toothbrush. It's no fun brushing your teeth with shaving lotion or shampoo! This plastic, cylindrical toothbrush holder keeps your brush clean and easy to locate.

Send: 50¢

Ask for: Toothbrush Holder

Write to: American Youth Hostels, Inc.
132 Spring St.
New York, NY 10012

Metal Mirror

This steel mirror is 4"-by-3" and weighs two ounces, perfect for sticking in your knapsack before you head off for that weekend camping trip. A small hole allows it to hang up. Totally unbreakable.

Send: $1.00

Ask for: Metal Mirror (No. 69-4893)

Write to: Eastern Mountain Sports
Vose Farm Rd.
Peterborough, NH 03458

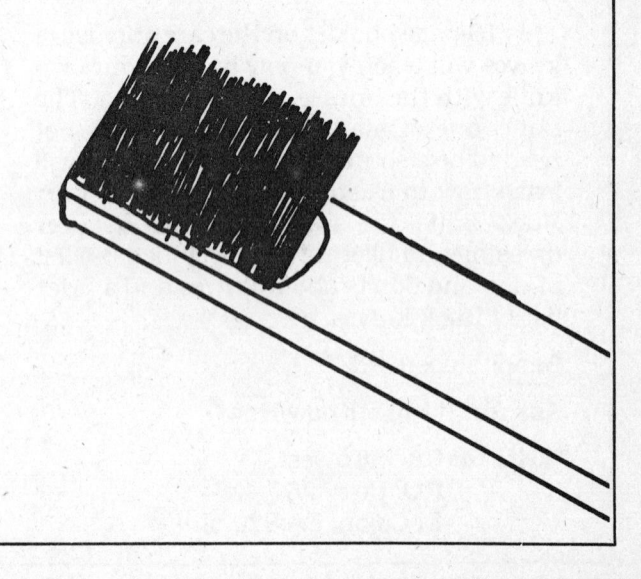

Map Case

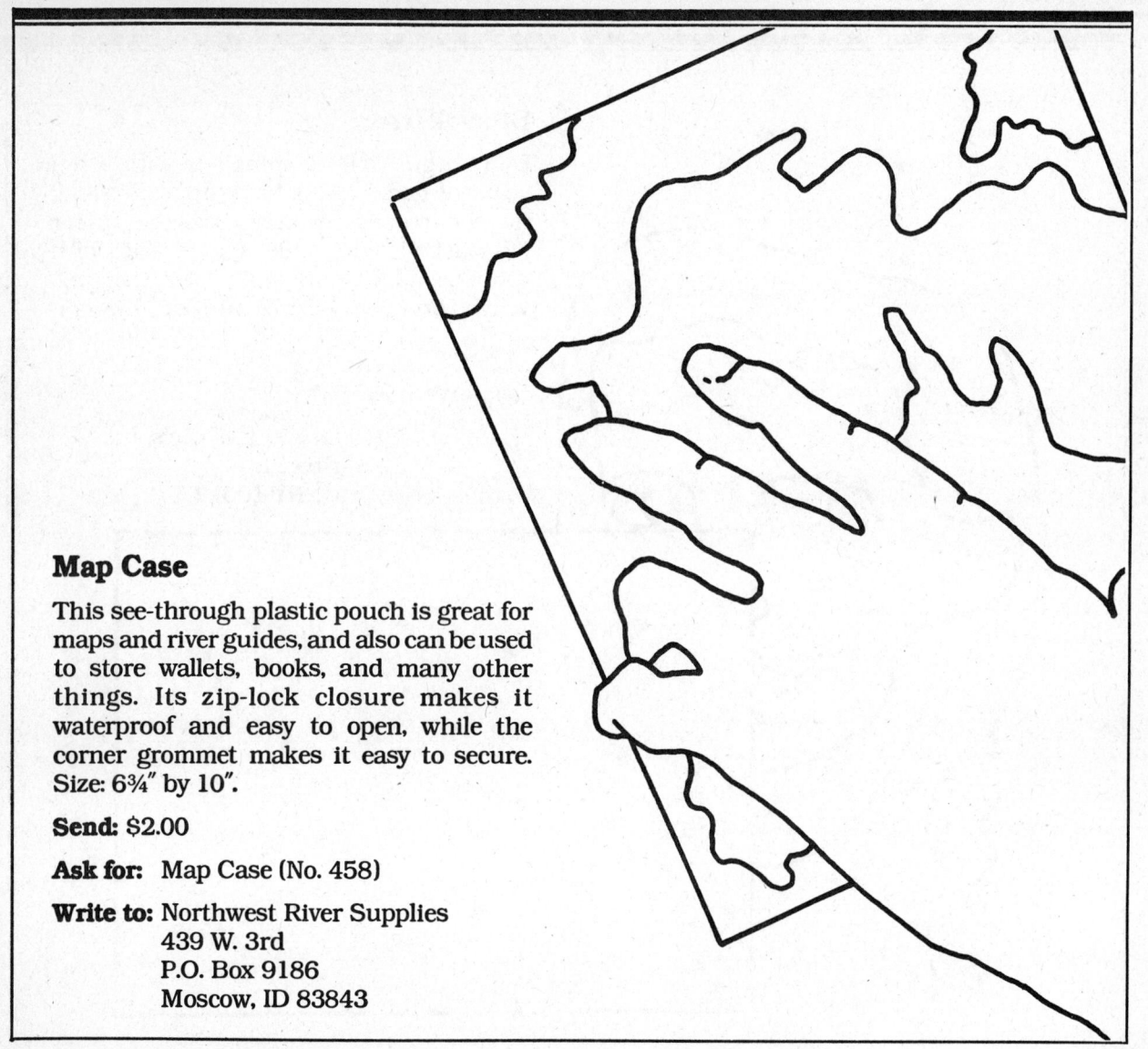

This see-through plastic pouch is great for maps and river guides, and also can be used to store wallets, books, and many other things. Its zip-lock closure makes it waterproof and easy to open, while the corner grommet makes it easy to secure. Size: 6¾" by 10".

Send: $2.00

Ask for: Map Case (No. 458)

Write to: Northwest River Supplies
439 W. 3rd
P.O. Box 9186
Moscow, ID 83843

Steel Mirror

Don't begin your camping trip with seven years of bad luck by breaking your small travel mirror. Carry an unbreakable mirror of polished steel. This square one, with rounded edges and a hole for hanging, weighs only 1.25 ounces and is 3" by 3½".

Send: $1.59

Ask for: Steel Mirror

Write to: American Youth Hostels, Inc.
132 Spring St.
New York, NY 10012

Day Hiking

For single-day trips into the forests or mountains, this little pamphlet will explain a lot. Tips and hints about footgear, animals, food, water, clothing, and following trails. You'll learn the easy and safe way to organize your pre-hike preparations so that you will have the most fun and return home safe and sound.

Send: 20¢

Ask for: "For the Day Hiker"

Write to: Adirondack Mountain Club, Inc.
172 Ridge St.
Glens Falls, NY 12801

Volcanic Ash Soap

Direct from Mount St. Helens, this light green, all-natural soap cleanses you with real volcanic ash. The particles of ash in each bar are smaller, rounder, and more uniform than the pumice found in many soaps. It's all biodegradable and gentle to your skin. Each box contains a small sample of volcanic ash that you can keep as a souvenir of that historic eruption of St. Helens.

Send: $1.95

Ask for: St. Helens Soap (No. 0630)

Write to: Early Winters, Ltd.
110 Prefontainte Place South
Seattle, WA 98104

Repair Kit

This small patch kit from Northwest River Supplies is handy—a 3"-by-4" piece of clear vinyl and a small tube of adhesive that will bond to all the vinyl products that NRS offers. Can be used on float bags, camera bags, and even the inflatable canoe/kayaks.

Send: 50¢ each

Ask for: NRS Patch Kit (No. 620)

Write to: Northwest River Supplies
439 W. 3rd
P.O. Box 9186
Moscow, ID 83843

VIII. Conservation

Save Your River!

Here is a brief guide to how citizens can organize to halt a destructive project on a nearby river. Learn what other agencies can help your cause, what committees and hearings in Washington should be contacted. In general, discover ways to build political strength and to develop alternatives to the proposed project. A list of publications, movies, and slide shows that may be of help is also included.

Send: 25¢

Ask for: "How to Save Your River"

Write to: Sierra Club
Information Services
530 Bush St.
San Francisco, CA 94108

Get Involved!

If you have wanted to take part in public meetings or write convincing letters to public policy makers but were always afraid that you didn't have enough knowledge about how policy is made, this little booklet will change all that. You can learn the various steps that are part of a decision-making process, learn how to participate in the process, and learn the criteria that are used. This booklet deals with ways to include fish and wildlife in national forest management plans. Read it and acquire the confidence that your voice can be heard—and listened to!

Send: 30¢

Ask for: "National Forest Management Plans: How to Include Fish and Wildlife"

Write to: Wildlife Management Institute
1000 Vermont Ave., N.W.
Washington, DC 20005

Conservation Practices

The National Outdoor Leadership School's material on conservation will show you how to reduce your impact on the backcountry you camp and hike through. More than just rules and guidelines, low-impact camping is a matter of attitudes and awareness. This pamphlet will give you both—the practical steps to make your human intrusion into the wilderness as nondestructive as possible and the ecological outlook that will keep your visit within the natural harmonies of the area.

Send: $2.00

Ask for: "NOLS Conservation Practices"

Write to: National Outdoor Leadership School
P.O. Box AA
Lander, WY 82520

Hunt the Dump

America is cluttered with hazardous waste sites. Citizen sleuthing and political activism can expose these dangerous areas. Average citizens do have power to shock public officials and the public at large into taking remedial action to clean up noxious sites that are threatening the nation's health as well as creating eyesores on the natural and urban landscapes. This four-step program will teach you and your neighbors how to get organized.

Send: 40¢

Ask for: "Hunt the Dump"

Write to: Sierra Club
Information Services
530 Bush St.
San Francisco, CA 94108

Safety in the Woods

Smokey the Bear and Woodsy Owl have been warning campers and hikers for years about the dangers of forest fires and pollution. Now you can display these colorful posters and stickers on your windows, car, tent, or boat. Send for this free kit of Smokey, Woodsy, and their forest friends and share their message with your friends. Give a hoot, don't pollute!

Send: a postcard

Ask for: Smokey and Woodsy posters and stickers

Write to: Information Officer
Chequamegon National Forest
Park Falls, WI 54552

Volunteers in Parks

If you like people and are concerned about the environment and have skills or talents you would like to share with others, being a volunteer in one of America's national parks may be the avocation for you. Anyone of any age can join in. Some of the areas with nonpaying jobs you might qualify for are: arts and crafts, living history, interpretation, history, archaeology, natural science, environmental study, resource management. Write for this brochure and discover a new way to spend your extra time in the great outdoors.

Send: a postcard

Ask for: "Volunteers in Parks"

Write to: (any National Park Service Regional Office) or
National Capital Regional Office
1100 Ohio Drive, S.W.
Washington, DC 20242

Safeguarding Wetlands

Wetlands and natural watercourses provide many valuable services to you and the environment. Learn how the 404 Permit Program works so that you can help safeguard these crucial areas of the ecosystem in your region of the nation. Learn what activities are destroying our nation's wetlands. Get involved in their protection.

Send: 30¢

Ask for: "Safeguarding Wetlands and Watercourses with 404"

Write to: Sierra Club
Information Services
530 Bush St.
San Francisco, CA 94108

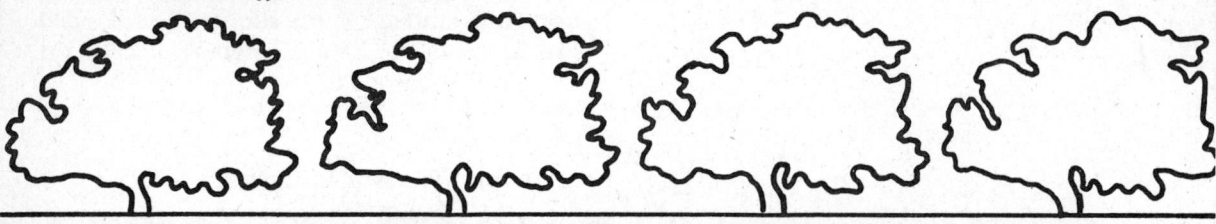

North American Wildlife Policy

This official document contains the report presented to the 37th North American Wildlife and Natural Resources Conference in Mexico City in 1973. The three major nations of North America set up a multidiscipline committee to study and advise on the wisest public policies for safeguarding the resources of North America. This is that report—a detailed presentation of uses and values of land, water, game, forest, range, wilderness, animals, guns, vehicles that will affect the natural landscape on the continent. Also included is the Leopold Report of 1930 on American Game Policy.

Send: $1.00

Ask for: The North American Wildlife Policy 1973

Write to: Wildlife Management Institute
1000 Vermont Ave., N.W.
Washington, DC 20005

Wilderness Misconceptions

Too many people have misconceptions about wilderness areas and so oppose the creation of further protected wilderness places. This handy pamphlet takes five of the common myths about wilderness areas and exposes them for what they are—myths and unfounded propaganda disseminated by people who would use our wilderness for exploitative purposes. Beef up your defense of the places you love by reading this pamphlet and learning how to enhance your arguments with convincing facts about wilderness.

Send: 20¢

Ask for: "Wilderness Myths and Misconceptions"

Write to: Sierra Club
Information Services
530 Bush St.
San Francisco, CA 94108

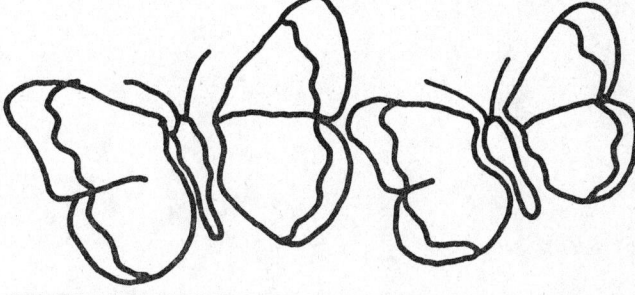

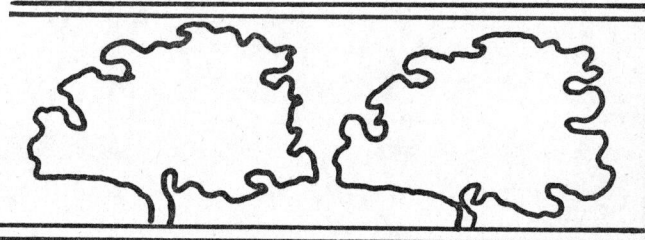

Teton Science School

The Grand Teton Science School was established to promote young people's interest in ecology and conservation. The goal of the school is to change people's attitudes toward the environment. The approach taken by the school is academic, utilizing scientific discipline. Students learn, not from classroom discussions, but from outdoor experiences in the wilderness that is the subject of their study. For more information, write for this brochure and course schedules.

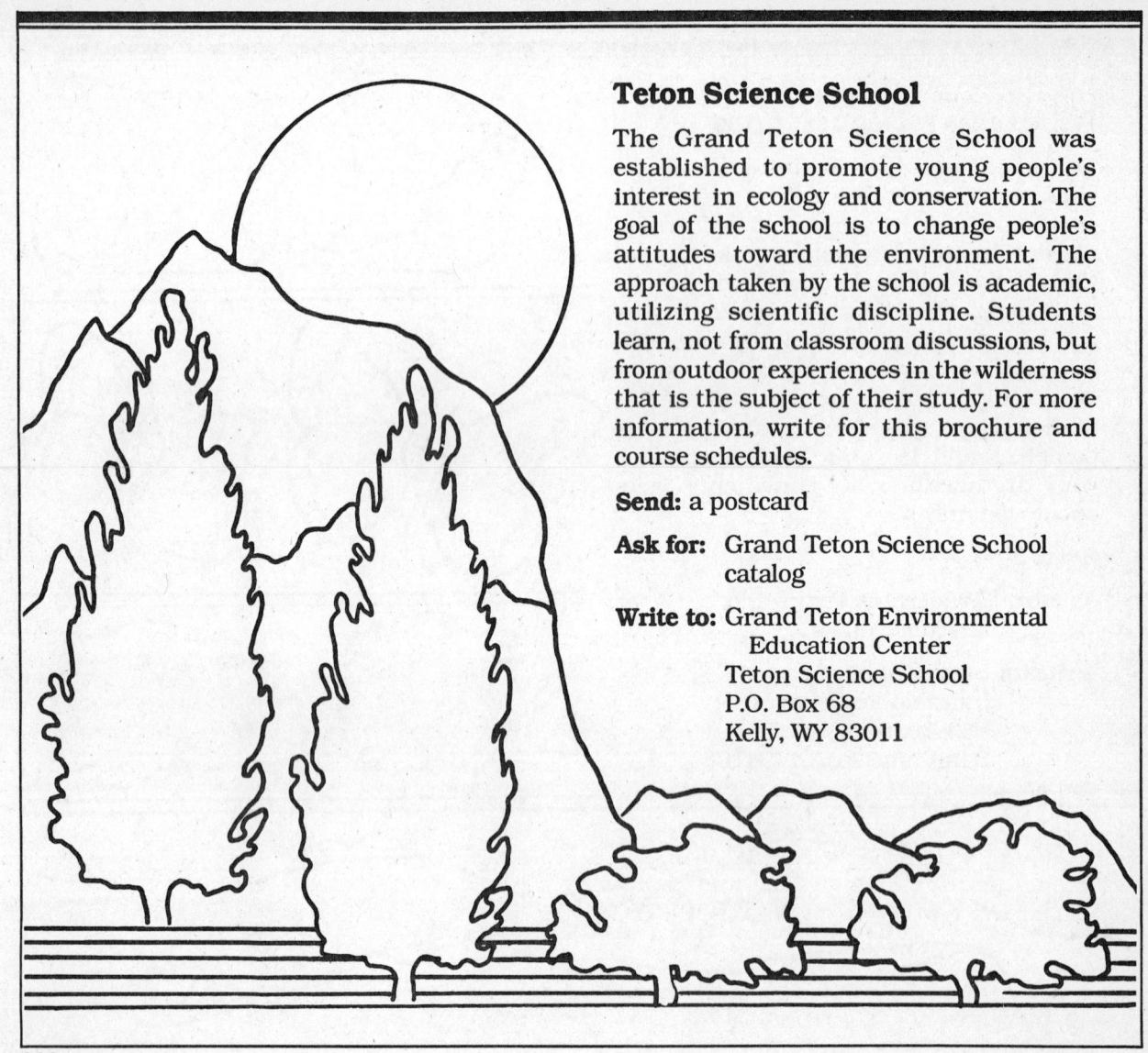

Send: a postcard

Ask for: Grand Teton Science School catalog

Write to: Grand Teton Environmental Education Center
Teton Science School
P.O. Box 68
Kelly, WY 83011

Principles of Ecology

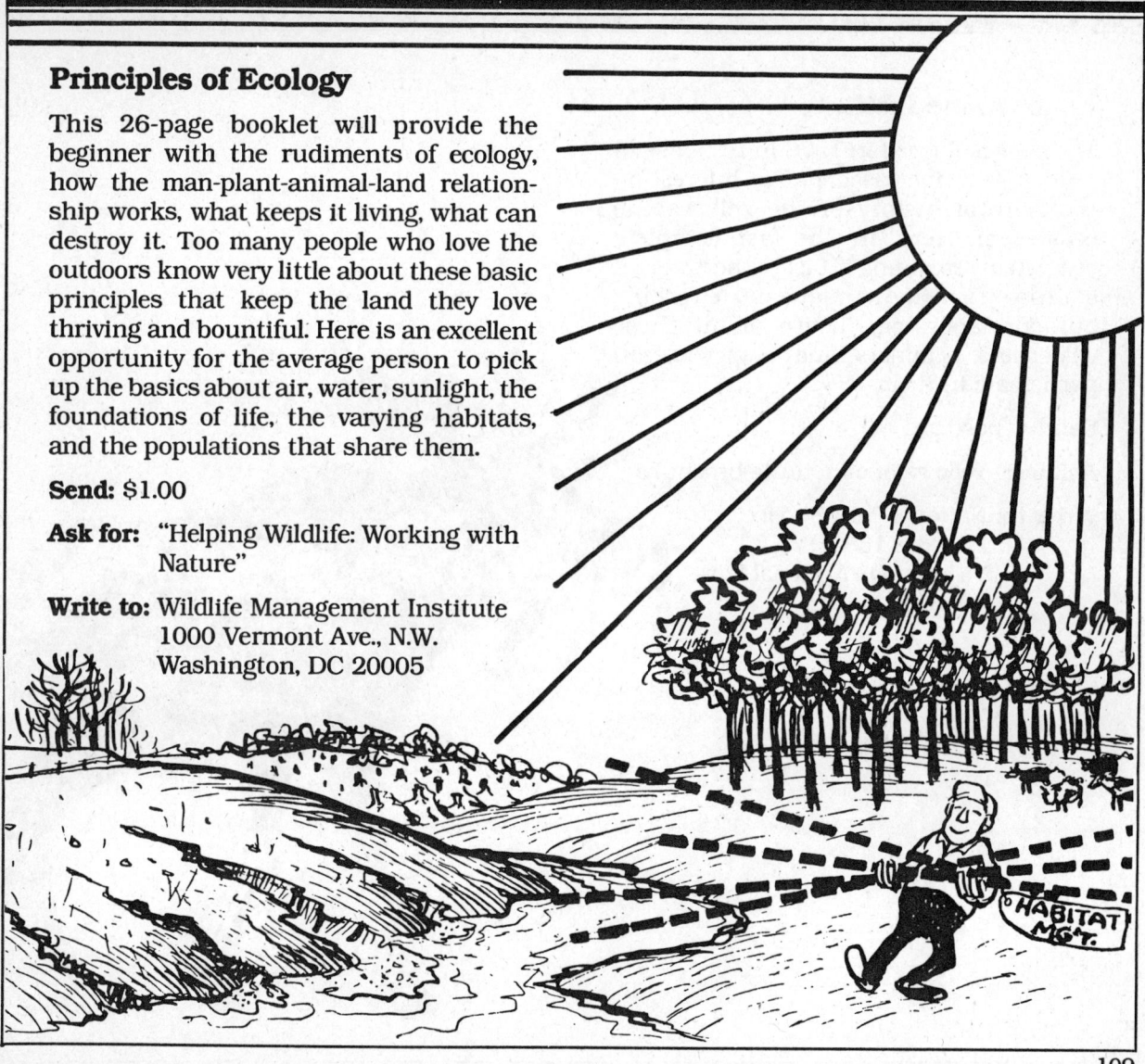

This 26-page booklet will provide the beginner with the rudiments of ecology, how the man-plant-animal-land relationship works, what keeps it living, what can destroy it. Too many people who love the outdoors know very little about these basic principles that keep the land they love thriving and bountiful. Here is an excellent opportunity for the average person to pick up the basics about air, water, sunlight, the foundations of life, the varying habitats, and the populations that share them.

Send: $1.00

Ask for: "Helping Wildlife: Working with Nature"

Write to: Wildlife Management Institute
1000 Vermont Ave., N.W.
Washington, DC 20005

Yellowstone Institute

The YI was formed in 1976 in response to dramatically increased public interest in the natural history of the Yellowstone ecosystem. Here, in the last complete ecosystem remaining intact in the lower 48 states, you will find a unique and rewarding outdoor laboratory. Learn about these wilderness seminars and how you can participate in them.

Send: a postcard

Ask for: Yellowstone Institute brochure

Write to: National Park Service
P.O. Box 168
Yellowstone National Park
WY 82190

Caring for Mountains

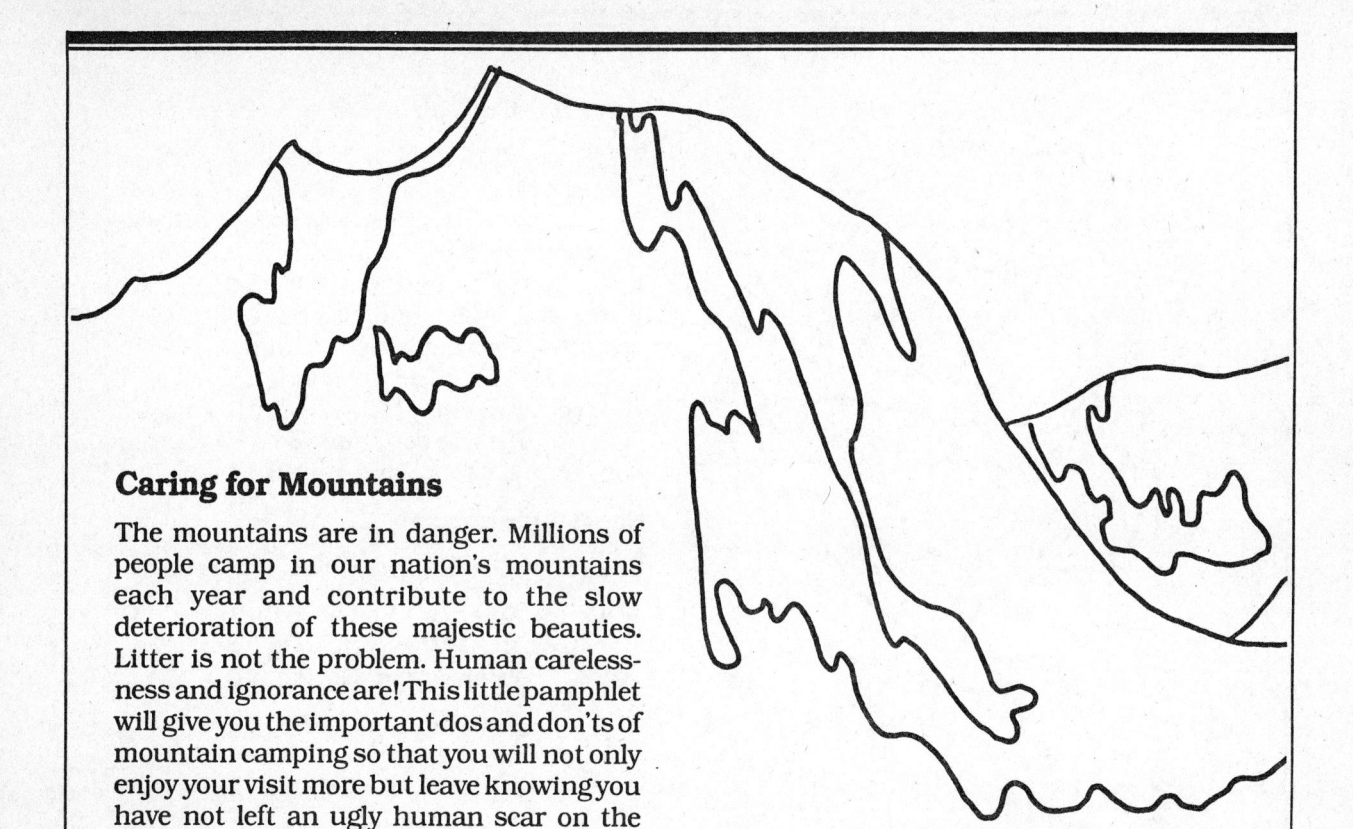

The mountains are in danger. Millions of people camp in our nation's mountains each year and contribute to the slow deterioration of these majestic beauties. Litter is not the problem. Human carelessness and ignorance are! This little pamphlet will give you the important dos and don'ts of mountain camping so that you will not only enjoy your visit more but leave knowing you have not left an ugly human scar on the mountain's face.

Send: 10¢

Ask for: "The Care and Enjoyment of Mountains"

Write to: Sierra Club
Information Services
530 Bush St.
San Francisco, CA 94108

Green America

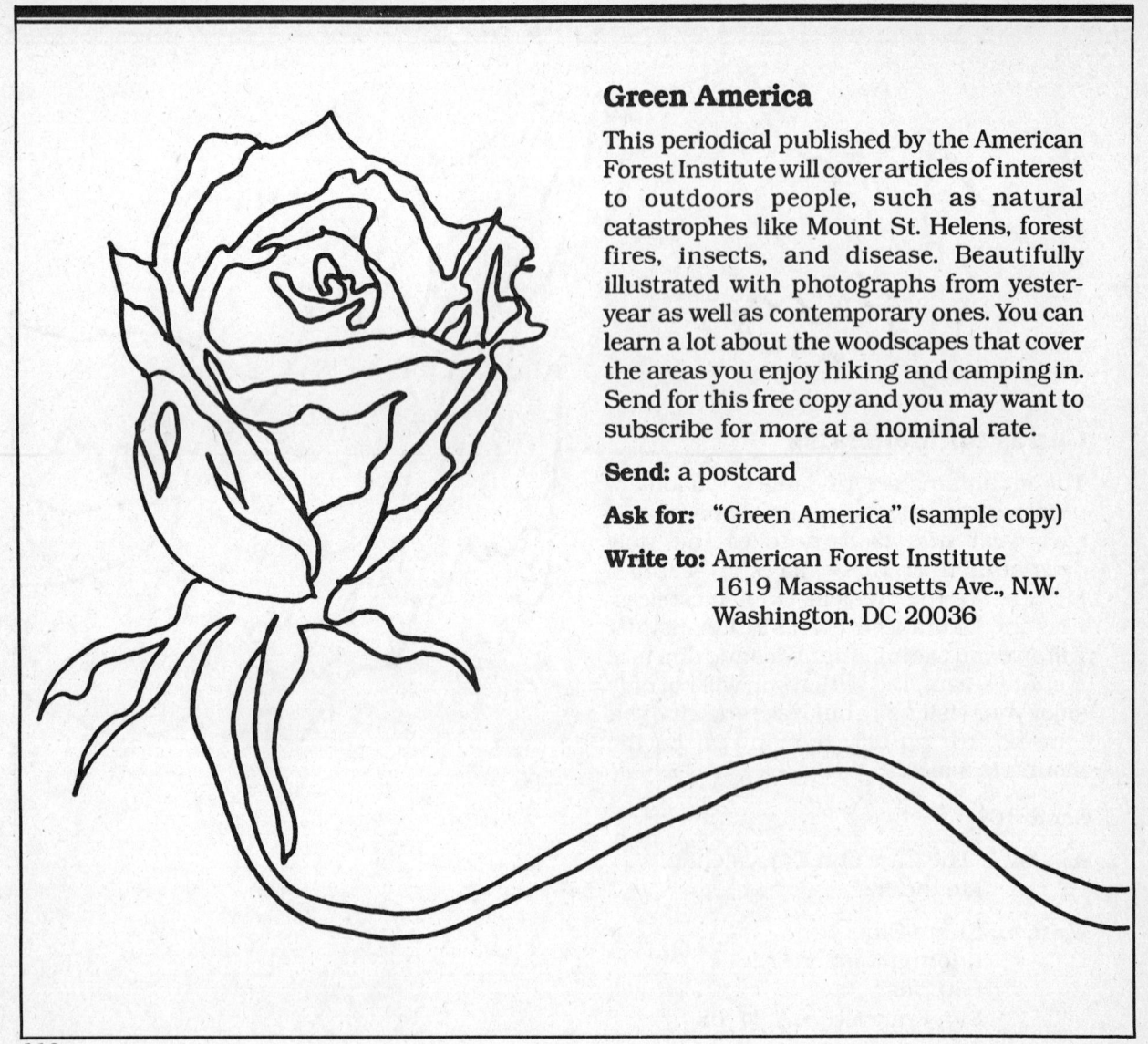

This periodical published by the American Forest Institute will cover articles of interest to outdoors people, such as natural catastrophes like Mount St. Helens, forest fires, insects, and disease. Beautifully illustrated with photographs from yesteryear as well as contemporary ones. You can learn a lot about the woodscapes that cover the areas you enjoy hiking and camping in. Send for this free copy and you may want to subscribe for more at a nominal rate.

Send: a postcard

Ask for: "Green America" (sample copy)

Write to: American Forest Institute
1619 Massachusetts Ave., N.W.
Washington, DC 20036

IX. Enjoying the Outdoors

Books About Yellowstone

Doing some research for your next trip to Yellowstone National Park? Or are you just an armchair explorer? Either way, this handy listing of books and pamphlets and maps about the area will be of use to you. Entries are organized into categories: general, plant life, geology, animal life, history.

Send: a postcard

Ask for: "Books, Pamphlets, and Maps About Yellowstone National Park"

Write to: Yellowstone Library and Museum Assoc.
P.O. Box 117
Yellowstone National Park
WY 82190

Wilderness Visuals

Bring the outdoors inside with posters, note cards, and slides from Wilderness Dreams. Six "I Like It Wild" posters depicting the wilderness, wild flowers, and wild animals in photographic realism. Or send your "wild" theme to friends on these 4½"-by-6½" note cards. For educational purposes, order photographic slides from this catalog that fully describes each scene.

Send: a self-addressed, stamped envelope

Ask for: brochure and price list

Write to: Wilderness Dreams
P.O. Box 4455
Shawnee Mission, KS 66204

Outdoors People Are Better Lovers

Not all of them, of course. But some. If you happen to be a better lover and you attribute your prowess to your particular or unusual outdoor activity, you may want to advertise it on an artistic glass plaque. Why not? Send for this pamphlet that lists all the various outdoor sports that you can have put on your plaque. There are plaques for hunters, fishermen, runners, horsemen, RV drivers, surfers, cyclists, and more. Are you a "better lover"?

Send: a self-addressed, stamped envelope

Ask for: "Artistry in Glass"

Write to: Artistry in Glass
332 Putnam Rd.
Union, NJ 07083

Wildlife Wall Graphics

For the outdoors people who like their indoors to look wild and natural, too, comes this brochure containing wildlife graphics silk-screened onto natural-colored cotton canvases and stretched on high-quality wooden bars. Owls, hawks, frogs, and lions are just some of the animals you can hang in your bedroom or den.

Send: 35¢

Ask for: catalog

Write to: Wildlife Wall Graphics
c/o Tin Man Studios
P.O. Box 1792
Madison, WI 53701

Books on the Great Outdoors

This catalog from Pruett Publishing Co. contains dozens of books that deal with many different aspects of the outdoors. Works on the national parks, railroads, and all aspects of Americana from urban histories of frontier cities to biographies of saints and scoundrels of the Old West. Many titles are new and others are backlisted.

Send: a postcard

Ask for: catalog

Write to: Pruett Publishing Co.
2928 Pearl St.
Boulder, CO 80302

Travel Games

This is a proven fun book for restless travelers. The book contains 32 pages of exciting highway games all family members can play. There are games dealing with highway signs, ecology, nature appreciation, types of homes, and more. Send for yours and make the miles on your next trip just whiz by!

Send: $1.00

Ask for: "Travel Games"

Write to: The Beavers
Star Route
Laporte, MN 56461

Treasure Hunting

Discover how you can find gold, silver, and treasure. Learn where valuable objects are most likely to turn up. This booklet will give you the facts and the secrets. You too can become a successful treasure hunter by using a modern electronic metal detector on beaches, old battlefields, ghost towns, and deserted fields.

Send: a postcard

Ask for: "Treasure Hunting Secrets"

Write to: Garrett Electronics
2814 National Dr.
Garland, TX 75041

Woodcarving

Here is a catalog for anyone interested in woodcarving, whittling, etching, and the related arts. Each line of tools is illustrated, with dimensions given. Sets of woodcarving tools will appeal to the beginner who has not yet invested in any tools. There is also a handy list of books dealing with all aspects of the wood sculpture arts.

Send: a postcard

Ask for: woodcraft catalog

Write to: Frank Mittermeier, Inc.
3577 E. Tremont Ave.
New York, NY 10465

Books, Books, Books!

This 84-page catalog lists all the books about our national parks. Arranged geographically, this complete mail-order catalog lets you find the books about the Indians, pioneers, animals, birds, flora, and history of the parks in the area of the country in which you are interested. A brief summary of each book accompanies it. Two indexes, one by park, the other by title, allow you to find books quickly and easily.

Send: $1.25

Ask for: National Park Service mail-order catalog

Write to: Eastern National Park and Monument Association
Apostle Island National Lakeshore
P.O. Box 729
Bayfield, WI 54814

The Story of Leather

From 500,000 years ago to the present day, people have been wearing leather on their feet. Leather making has really come a long way! The new "king" of leather is pigskin, and this skin, although difficult to remove from the animal, has led to a flourishing business in the shoe industry. Read about the history of leather and leather shoes in this fun little book and know more about the basic material that you walk on every day. Also included are five hints for making the proper shoe size selection.

Send: a postcard

Ask for: "Let's Look at Leather"

Write to: Wolverine World Wide
Dept. B
Rockford, MI 49531

Books on Grand Teton

If you are interested in the Grand Tetons—the national park or the thousands of acres of wilderness, golden sunrises, bald eagles, moose, and rivers that comprise this wildlife legacy—this book list from the Grand Teton Natural History Association will suggest guides and maps, history, wildlife, geology, mountaineering, and selected climbs in the Teton range. Included are a price list and a convenient order form.

Send: a postcard

Ask for: Grand Teton publications list

Write to: Grand Teton Natural History Assoc.
Grand Teton National Park
Moose, WY 83012

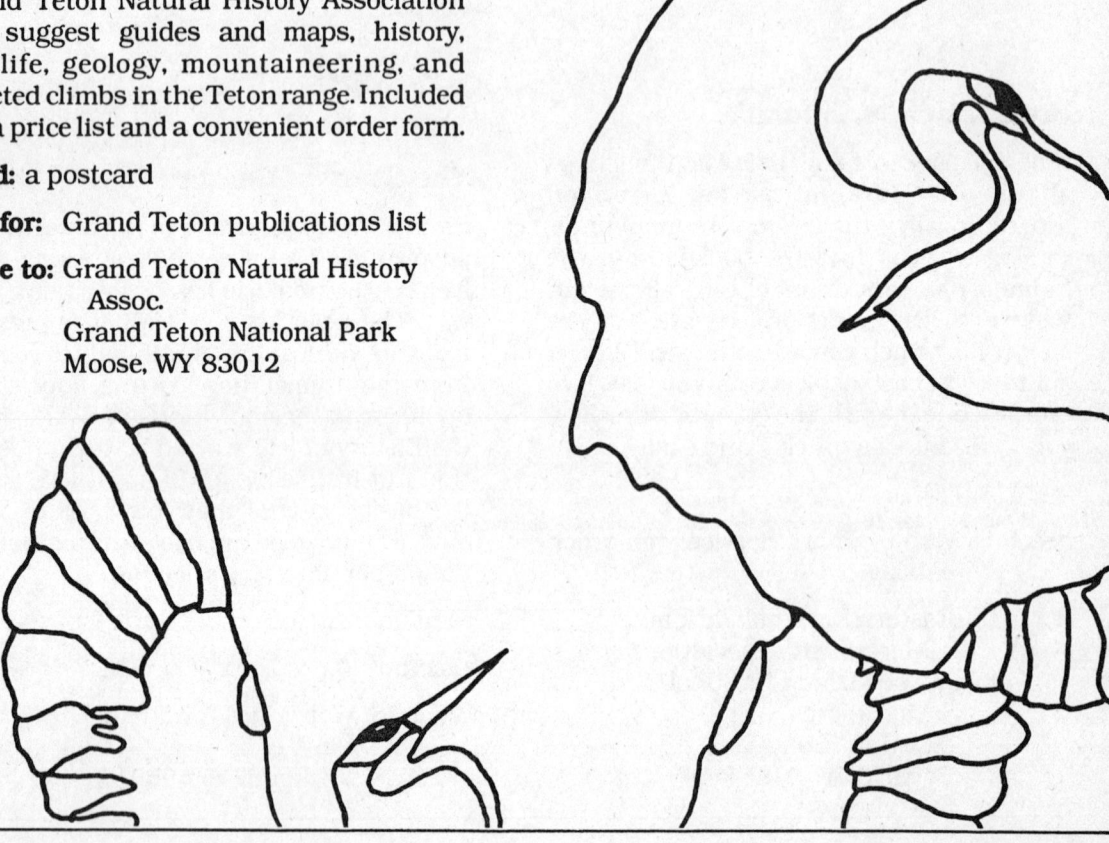

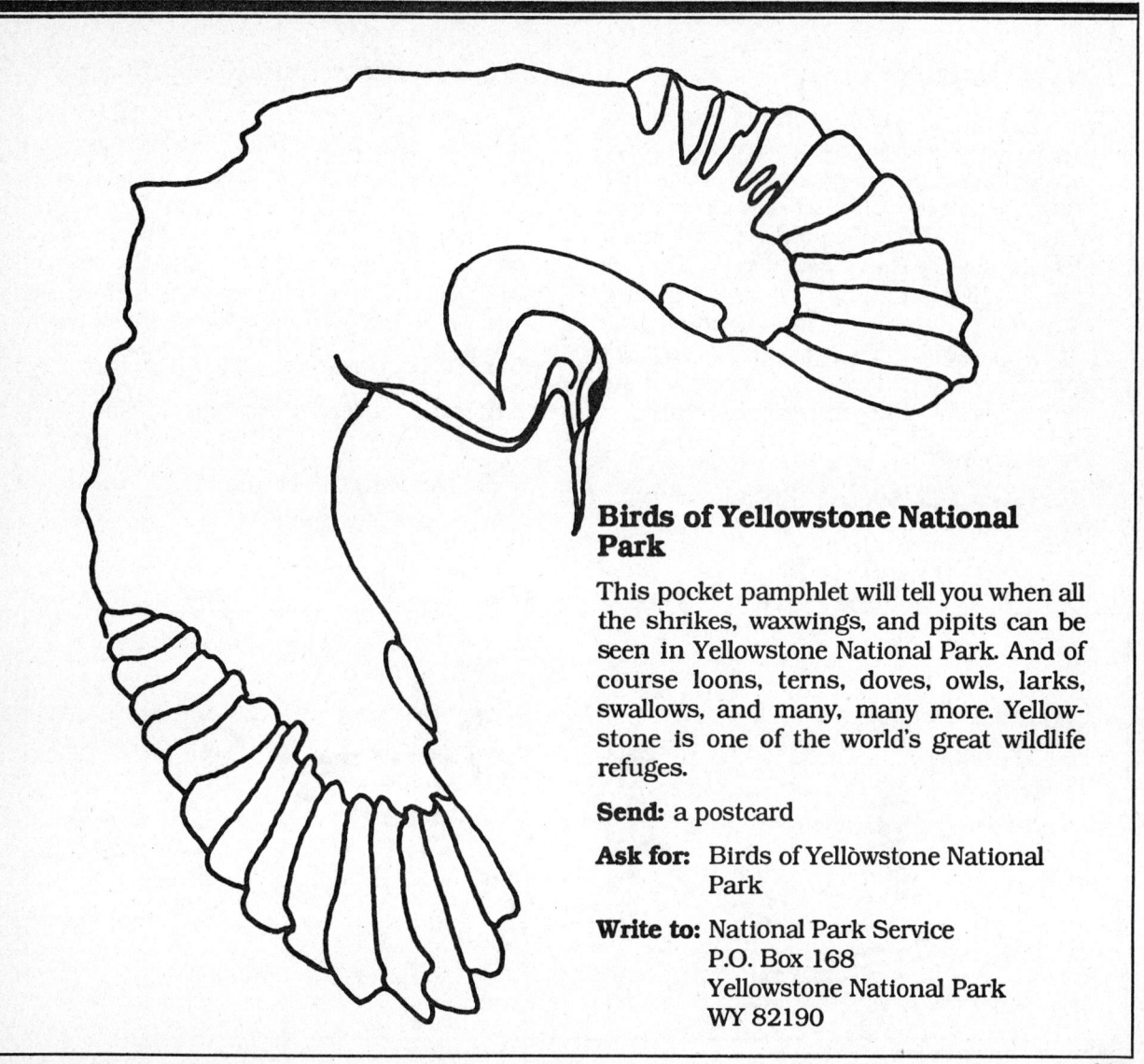

Birds of Yellowstone National Park

This pocket pamphlet will tell you when all the shrikes, waxwings, and pipits can be seen in Yellowstone National Park. And of course loons, terns, doves, owls, larks, swallows, and many, many more. Yellowstone is one of the world's great wildlife refuges.

Send: a postcard

Ask for: Birds of Yellowstone National Park

Write to: National Park Service
P.O. Box 168
Yellowstone National Park
WY 82190

Metal Detectors

Beachcombing, ghost-towning, and hunting for coins, treasure, and battlefield relics are just some of the outdoor activities that have been revolutionized by electronics. Foremost among the producers of metal detectors is the Garrett Electronics Co. You can receive their giant catalog and consumer buyer's guide free. Along with the latest models of metal detectors you'll get other literature that will make you a more knowledgeable modern treasure hunter.

Send: a postcard

Ask for: metal detector catalog

Write to: Garrett Electronics
2814 National Dr.
Garland, TX 75041

Modern Electronic Prospecting

If you are the owner of a VLF/TR metal detector, this handy instructional booklet will give you pointers on how to make the best use of it. You'll learn how to use coaxial and coplanar search coils, how to analyze samples, and how to search in both dry and wet places. Become a better treasure hunter and you'll find gold and silver the easy way!

Send: a postcard

Ask for: "Modern Electronic Prospecting with the VLF/TR Metal Detector"

Write to: Garrett Electronics
2814 National Dr.
Garland, TX 75041

Yellowstone Wildlife Car Game

Driving with children through Yellowstone National Park? Here's a fun little game that will keep the whole family occupied for hours. Place a check mark near the picture of each bird or mammal you see and score 10 points for each mark. See who can spot the most wildlife!

Send: a postcard

Ask for: "Wildlife Check List"

Write to: National Park Service
P.O. Box 168
Yellowstone National Park
WY 82190

Books for Outdoors People

If you need guidebooks for your next trip or just like to read about nature and outdoor activities, you don't have to browse for hours in a library or bookstore to learn what is available. These book lists cover almost every aspect of outdoor recreation, including ballooning, kayaking, rafting, ice climbing, and scuba diving, in addition to the more popular sports like backpacking, canoeing, and hiking.

Send: a self-addressed #10 envelope with postage to handle two ounces (per list)

Ask for: "Backpacking/Hiking/Walking"
"Rock/Ice/Mountain Climbing"
"Bike Racing/Touring"
"Canoeing/Kayaking/Rafting"
"Cross Country/Downhill Skiing"
"First Aid/Search and Rescue"

Write to: Burke's Outdoor Recreational
Book Supply
7 Bluff Point Rd.
Northport, NY 11768

More Books for Outdoors People

If you're looking for a glossy brochure that lists the latest and the classics on outdoor activities, this free thing from Knapp's Outdoor Books is just the ticket. Books are arranged topically, with a brief description of each book, including the price. In addition to the usual activities, there are sections on cookbooks, Alaska, and horses.

Send: a postcard

Ask for: catalog

Write to: Knapp's Outdoor Books
P.O. Box 2201
Jackson, WY 83001

Treasure Hunting Clubs

Form your own treasure hunting club with this booklet that tells you everything you need to know about electing officers, getting community assistance, creating good relationships with local dealers and manufacturers, appointing committees, even choosing a club name. You'll also learn of the wide variety of club activities that your club may want to sponsor, such as a library, raffles, and hunting classes for beginners. Not only will you learn how to organize your club, you'll learn the tricks of keeping it going.

Send: a postcard

Ask for: "How to Form a Treasure Club"

Write to: Garrett Electronics
2814 National Dr.
Garland, TX 75041

Passports to the Great Outdoors

As you may already know, many parks, forests, wildlife areas, and campsites charge nominal entrance or usage fees. Here are two passports that will reduce these fees or eliminate them altogether. The Golden Eagle Passport for people under 62 is a yearly pass to many outdoor places. The Golden Age Passport is for people over 62 and is good for a lifetime. Write for more information on how to obtain yours.

Send: a postcard

Ask for: Golden Eagle/Golden Age Passports

Write to: Office of Information
USDA-Forest Service
Pacific Southwest Region
630 Sansome St.
San Francisco, CA 94111

Learn Mountaineering

To go mountain climbing like the professionals, you have to learn from the professionals. What to do amidst peaks, crags, ravines, and glaciers is not innate knowledge. Take a professional course in mountaineering and learn how to climb those rocks safely and expertly. Many skills are needed to really experience and enjoy the thrill of the high ranges. Write for this introduction and catalog to the seminars and guide services offered by the Palisade School of Mountaineering.

Send: a postcard

Ask for: brochure

Write to: Palisade School of
Mountaineering
P.O. Box 694
Bishop, CA 93514

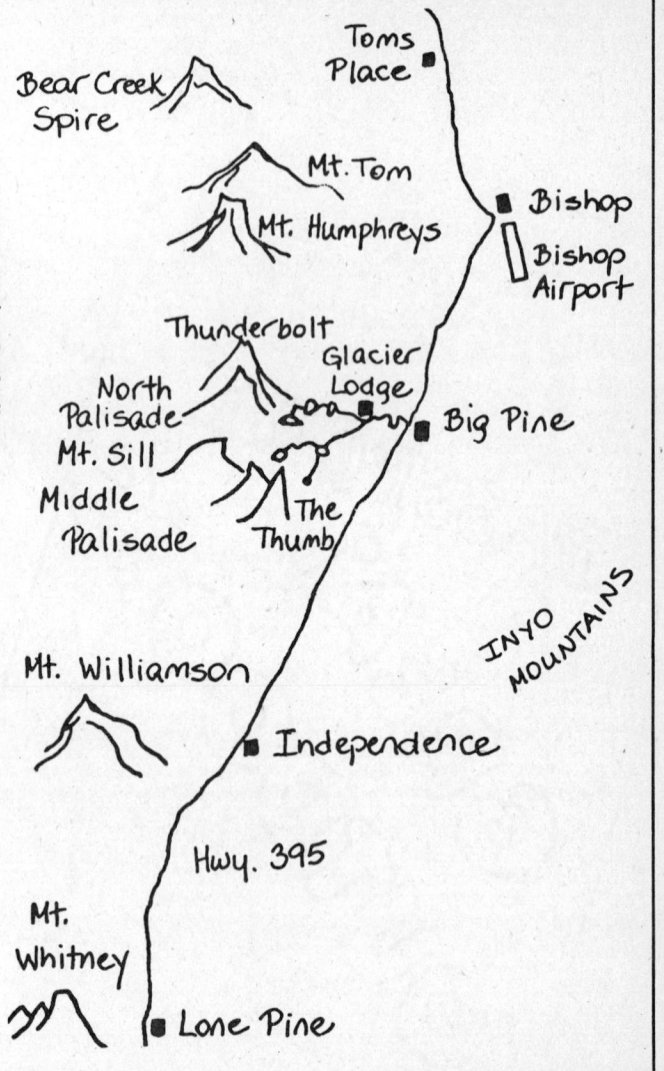

Outdoor Annual

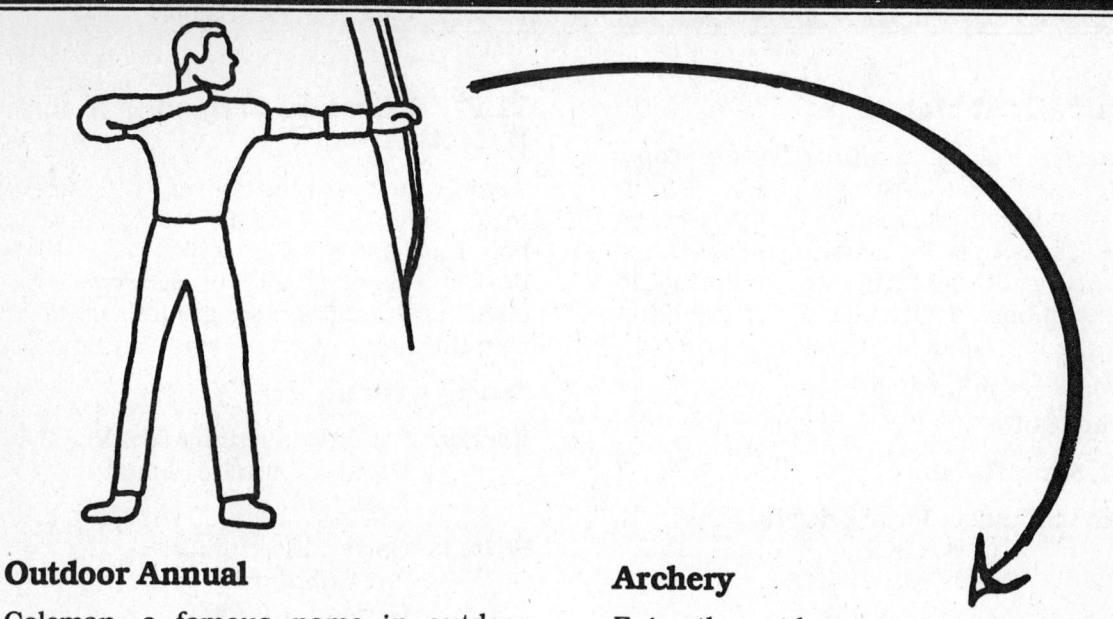

Coleman, a famous name in outdoor equipment, publishes an annual magazine of interesting and informative articles for people who love the outdoors. Topics range from boats to motorcycles, fishing to tenting and backpacking, canoeing to cooking hints. Many articles deal with stretching your dollars and finding cheaper ways to invest in outdoor equipment.

Send: $1.50

Ask for: "Outdoor Annual"

Write to: The Coleman Co.
250 N. St. Francis
Wichita, KS 67201

Archery

Enjoy the outdoors even more with both gun and bow. This colorful new catalog from Bear Archery is just what the two-season hunter needs. Containing not only the most complete archery line available, the catalog also features a series of Fred Bear's personal bow-hunting tips, great for novice and veteran alike.

Send: a postcard

Ask for: catalog

Write to: Bear Archery
Rural Rt. 4
4600 S.W. 41st Blvd.
Gainesville, FL 32601

Knife-Craft Materials

Here is a catalog and price list for people interested in all aspects of knives and cutlery. Kits to make your own knives, as well as listings for finished products for hunting or cooking. Complete blade descriptions are given. The $1.00 handling charge is refundable should you place an order for any item.

Send: $1.00

Ask for: catalog

Write to: Indian Ridge Traders
P.O. Box 869
Royal Oak, MI 48068

VLF/TR Ground Canceling Metal Detectors

If you know nothing or very little about metal detectors, here is your chance to begin a fascinating hobby. This little booklet will answer all your basic questions about scanning speeds, ground minerals, coin hunting, detection depth, and more.

Send: a postcard

Ask for: "An Introduction to the VLF/TR Ground Canceling Metal Detector"

Write to: Garrett Electronics
2814 National Dr.
Garland, TX 75041

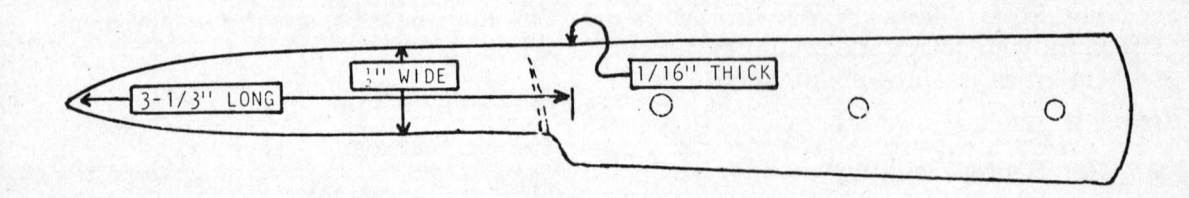

X. Tips for the Trailwise

Tips for the Trailwise

1. Be prepared for extremes in weather. Always carry extra clothing and rain gear.

2. Bring along more food than you think you'll need in case of an emergency.

3. Notify a friend or relative about your plans and expected time of return.

4. If visiting a state or national park or forest, make your plans known to the rangers, particularly if you're to be traveling into wilderness areas.

5. Always carry a first-aid kit, and know how to use it.

6. Never hike alone, especially in deep wilderness.

7. Keep your distance from wild animals. Even the cutest chipmunk can inflict serious injury.

8. Keep to your own limits. Overdoing is hazardous to your health.

9. Always inexcusable in a pristine setting is the slightest trace of human litter. Bring a heavy-duty group litter bag, or supply each person with a small one for all nonbiodegradable materials such as toilet paper and aluminum packaging (it takes 32 years for a piece of foil to decompose). And while you're at it, why not pick up any litter left by others.

10. Keep to designated trails and campgrounds, obeying all resource-management regulations.

11. Admire, but don't pick wild flowers. The saying goes, "Take only pictures, leave only footprints."

12. Leave your radio at home and enjoy the natural songs of birds, wind, and water.

13. Build campfires only where permitted, gathering only dead, fallen twigs and branches. Better yet, bring a stove and leave fallen wood where it lies.

14. Bathe, wash dishes, and relieve yourself well away from all water sources.

15. Pets aren't allowed in many designated wildernesses. They can disturb wildlife and other campers. So think twice before you bring along old faithful.

16. Enjoy yourself!

Jeffrey Weiss is an avid sportsman with a particular interest in backpacking